MARKET

HELL RAZOR

HELL RAZOR

The Autobiography of
NEIL RUDDOCK
with DAVE SMITH

CollinsWillow
An Imprint of HarperCollinsPublishers

Dave Smith, who collaborated with Neil Ruddock on this book, was editor of *Shoot* magazine until 1997. He currently works as a freelance soccer writer and match reporter. He has co-written autobiographies of Trevor Steven, Gary Stevens and Dave Beasant, and is the author of several soccer coaching and fitness books.

First published in hardback in 1999
by CollinsWillow
an imprint of HarperCollins*Publishers*
London

First published in paperback in 2000

The HarperCollins website address is:
www.fireandwater.com

1 3 5 7 9 8 6 4 2

A CIP catalogue record for this book
is available from the British Library

ISBN 0 00 218910 0

Printed and bound in Great Britain by Clays Ltd, St Ives plc

Photographic acknowledgements
Action Images 3br, 6b, 8t, 11t, 13t, 13b, 15t; Allsport 2br, 4t, 4bl, 6t, 7tl, 10br, 11c, 12b, 13c, 15m; Colorsport 3tl, 3tr, 4br, 5br, 6c; Empics 2bl, 10t, 10bl, 12c; PA News 7b, 9c, 11b, 15c; Popperfoto 2t, 3bl, 12t.
All other photographs courtesy of Neil Ruddock.

Contents

To Sarah, Josh and Millie

CHAPTER ONE

Never a Dull Moment

As I look back at my 15-year career as a professional footballer, I find it hard to believe the incredible changes that have taken place in the sport since it all began for me as a starry-eyed teenager with Millwall.

For starters, my daily routine as a Premiership player has altered dramatically, certainly in recent years, what with the influx of foreign players and coaches and the introduction of fitness advisors, dieticians, sports psychologists and the like. As far as preparation for matches is concerned it is, literally, a whole new ball game and we are treated more like athletes than just footballers these days.

Financially, too, things have moved on in leaps and bounds as football has become a massive, international business. The rewards for top players are so much greater, but then so are the pressures and demands in a game that has become more than a sport; much more. Even at a traditional, 'family club' like West Ham the expectation level has soared as the club attempts to compete with the likes of Manchester United, Arsenal and Chelsea in the world of high finance.

One thing that hasn't changed, however, is my love for the game and the enjoyment I continue to extract from my life as a professional footballer in the best league in the world. Whether I have been on the most incredible highs – like the time I won my one and only cap for England – or enduring the depressing lows which inevitably follow, I have never lost sight of the fact that I am being well paid for doing something I love; something I dreamed of as a kid. It has been an eventful journey which has taken me from South London and the Lions' Den to the East End and my current club West Ham – via Spurs, Southampton and Liverpool – and while the trophy cabinet at home might not exactly be bulging, the memory bank certainly is. Full of stories, anecdotes and experiences which still make me smile – although there are some antics I will reveal in this book which actually make me cringe. I'm certainly no angel, hence the title of my autobiography, and like most people in any walk of life, I've made mistakes and done things which have earned me, rightly or wrongly, a reputation as a tearaway.

Like the time I crossed swords with my old Spurs boss David Pleat whom I remember vividly telling me that I would probably make a better security guard than a footballer. I was a 17-year-old new boy at White Hart Lane at the time but, already, revelling in the high jinks that invariably make up a pre-season tour. It was perhaps not the kind of impression I should have been making so soon after joining my first 'big club', but that's the way it was when a group of lads got together. Still is, to a certain extent. That's not to say I haven't taken my football seriously throughout my career; no manager I have ever played for during my time at Millwall, Spurs,

Southampton, Liverpool and West Ham could question my commitment to those clubs or contest the fact that I have always given 100 per cent on the field.

Supporters at my previous clubs still come up to me and tell me what a good job I did for their favourite team, praising me for the whole-hearted way I approach the game. That means a lot to me. But while I have always recognised that football has given me a damned good living, I have also been of the mind that whatever happens in my career, I'm going to enjoy every minute of it. Yes, I take my job seriously but, as everyone keeps reminding me, a footballer's career is a short one so my philosophy has always been 'make the most of it, son'. And I have.

Okay, so there have been times when my commitment to the cause has resulted in me getting involved in a few scrapes, both on and off the field, and earning a reputation as one of football's wild men who has over-stepped the mark on too many occasions for some people's liking. But, while David Pleat's remarks might not have been too complimentary, I don't see myself as a problem player. Sure, I'm a big bloke and I can take care of myself, but I've never consciously gone out of my way to cause trouble or hit someone without good reason. I used to be something of a hot-head (although I like to think I've calmed down a bit in recent years) and was prone to over-reacting when the red mist descended, but my disciplinary record is not that bad. A few red cards here, a lot more yellow cards there, but I'm certainly not in the Vinnie Jones league when it comes to sendings off and suspensions. I play the game hard, but I also believe I play it fair. And if anyone wants to argue about that…!

I'm the first to admit I've done some stupid things in

my time and I'm not particularly proud of my involvement in certain incidents down the years; like the time I head-butted Craig Short and was sent off during my Southampton career, or when I had a ruck with then team-mate Robbie Fowler in my Liverpool days. But these things happen in football, although I'm sure my first ever manager George Graham has a little chuckle to himself whenever he reads or hears stories about his one-time protégé Neil Ruddock landing himself in a spot of bother yet again. Because it was George, then an up-and-coming boss with Millwall, who gave me the mother of all rollickings after I'd had a brush with the law during my time as a teenage apprentice at The Den. Although I was released by the police with just a caution, the worst bit was still to come … facing the wrath of George. I was bricking it as I made my way towards the manager's office the next morning because, even in those early days, George Graham was not a man to trifle with.

He let me know in no uncertain terms what he thought of my behaviour and I was severely warned about my future conduct. I learned a valuable lesson that day and, thanks to George, I've enjoyed a trouble-free career ever since! Ironically, after punishing me by putting me on ground duty (cleaning the stadium, painting, that sort of stuff), George gave me my senior debut a couple of weeks later and then proceeded to act as my first ever 'agent', negotiating my £70,000 transfer to Tottenham at the end of that season. I hadn't even played a League game for Millwall by that stage, just a couple of Freight Rover Trophy run-outs, but he still got the price he wanted – and got me a better deal than I was originally offered. But then George has always been good with money!

That was a fantastic opportunity for me and although

I only made nine first team appearances in two and a half years at White Hart Lane, the experience stood me in good stead for the rest of my career. Working with the likes of Glenn Hoddle, Chris Waddle and Ossie Ardiles was a dream come true. And it was during this first spell with Spurs that David Pleat came out with his immortal assessment of my ability a few days into a pre-season tour of Sweden. He'd insisted on all the lads being in bed by a certain time on a Friday night because we'd got a game the following day but his advice fell on deaf ears and all the players, including the senior and sensible pros like Hoddle and Waddle, sneaked out of the hotel at about 9pm to find the local disco. As a 17-year-old rookie it was my job to order the drinks and fetch them from the bar for the more seasoned campaigners. Since the well-paid members of the squad were buying me drinks to do so, I was happy to oblige. It wasn't a particularly boozy affair but, just as I'd ordered up another round of drinks, I turned round to discover that all my team-mates had left suddenly and just one recognisable face remained … that of David Pleat. As I stood there, shame-faced and pints in hand, the manager looked me straight in the face and with a wagging finger said, 'When you finish playing football young man, which is going to be very soon I feel, you'll make a very good security guard'.

It wasn't too long after my run-in with Pleat that I was on my way back to Millwall – although it had nothing to do with the incident – where I spent only a few months before signing for Southampton, the club I still describe to people as the best I ever played for. A homely club, a friendly club and arguably the place where I had the greatest fun of my career in four incident-packed years on the South Coast. One of the real thrills was playing alongside my ultimate footballing hero Terry Hurlock, a wonderful and crazy character who perhaps didn't have the ability of some but whose attitude was absolutely spot on. Terry, of course, was a Millwall legend and some early advice he gave me made a lasting impression on me as a kid learning the ropes. 'Tel' was also one of the proudest men ever to pull on an England shirt, albeit for the 'B' team, and I would put him in my all-time great XI … every time. When Terry stopped playing he ran his own pub and whenever there was an England international match on television, he would insist on *everyone* in the place standing to attention for the National Anthem, or else! You didn't argue with Tel. That was typical of his patriotism and his passion for the game.

It was during my time at The Dell that I first came across the remarkable goal-scoring talent of a certain Alan Shearer and the immense individual ability of Matt Le Tissier who, next to Glenn Hoddle, is the most gifted player I've been privileged to play alongside. And there have been a few, I can tell you. I became great mates with Shearer, who didn't acquire the nickname 'Shocksy' for nothing, but not before I'd been involved in a boozy incident which almost ended the career of the goal-scoring sensation before it had really begun. More about that later. As we all know, Alan has gone on to great things and more than lived up to his early potential, scoring goals for fun and achieving the ultimate accolade of captaining his country. That is what a lot of players dream of and I was no exception, although my international career hardly deserves a mention alongside that of my old Southampton pal. I did win one full

England cap, thanks to Terry Venables, but my most vivid England memories still come from the days when I played for the England youth team during my first spells with Millwall and Spurs.

It was during one particular tour of South America in 1987 that I landed myself in a spot of bother by getting sent off twice in two successive internationals. And all this after the whole squad had been warned, by coach Bobby Robson no less, to be on our best behaviour after the national team had been 'disgraced' by the World Cup sending-off of Ray Wilkins in Mexico the previous year. Nice one, Razor.

I don't think my early disciplinary problems affected my international career after that, although I would like to have won more than one England cap, of which I'm supremely proud nonetheless. As I said, that honour was given to me by Terry Venables who was originally my boss at Spurs and a man I have so much respect and admiration for. I've said it before and I stand by it, I would die for the man. That's how much I think of him. And that is why I made my own personal protest against his dismissal from White Hart Lane by chairman Alan Sugar who, it's fair to say, I didn't have the same respect for. Still don't, in fact. Venables, like Graeme Souness at Liverpool later, was my sort of manager. Both were players' bosses who stood by their team no matter what the circumstances and it was a pleasure to work under them.

I had signed for Graeme Souness as much as Liverpool Football Club when I left Spurs. In fact, I'd turned down approaches from some of the biggest managers in the game purely and simply because I wanted to play for him. When it became clear I was leaving White Hart

Lane, I'd arranged to have talks, not just with Souness, but Kenny Dalglish at Blackburn, Glenn Hoddle at Chelsea and Kevin Keegan at Newcastle. Not a bad selection of clubs or bosses from which to choose your next career move. After initial talks, impressive ones too, with Dalglish, I spoke to Kenny's former Liverpool pal Souness the following day. The others never had a look-in after that. I just knew I wanted to play for Liverpool the club, and for Souness the manager in particular. Our partnership may have been short-lived, but I have a lot of happy recollections of another man I totally admired; and of my spell on Merseyside in general.

I was deeply saddened by Souness's departure from Liverpool, a club he loved and where he desperately wanted to succeed, and I still stand by what I thought at the time that the club's top brass dropped an almighty clanger in ending the contract of a man I confidently believe would have made Liverpool bigger than Manchester United. He could have achieved everything at Anfield that Alex Ferguson has achieved at Old Trafford ... and more. But if Souness's exit was disappointing, it was nothing compared to the heartbreak of being told, on my birthday no less, that I would not be playing in the 1996 FA Cup Final against Manchester United. Roy Evans, Graeme's successor, was widely regarded as 'one of the nicest men in football', but he broke my heart that day. And they say that big boys don't cry.

Playing for Liverpool was a great experience though, and did provide me with my only medal of note to date (in the Coca Cola Cup in 1995), although I did go through a very difficult time towards the end when a series of injuries sidelined me for lengthy spells during which, by my own admission, I went off the rails somewhat.

The last year or so at Anfield was a bit disappointing because I couldn't command a regular first-team place so, after a brief loan spell with QPR, the chance to return to London with West Ham was simply too good an opportunity to turn down.

The funny thing is that it was me who actually contacted Harry Redknapp, whose son Jamie is a close friend. Jamie asked his dad to come to my rescue after he'd hinted to me that he would like to sign me. 'If you want to get out of Anfield and come to West Ham, just give me a call,' I remember him saying. So I did. Harry was great but he was slightly worried about the fact I was a little overweight after a lengthy spell of inactivity and he went on record at the time as saying 'a fit Neil Ruddock is one of the best defenders in the country; an unfit Neil Ruddock is no good to us.'

I'd like to think I've been a good buy for him and given him good service so far, although Harry had cause for concern when I was arrested, along with Trevor Sinclair, as a result of a well-publicised, but misinterpreted incident on the afternoon of the club's 1998 Christmas party, which I helped organise, you'll be surprised to learn. Needless to say, it was a boozy affair and an unfortunate incident which got completely out of hand took place and resulted in both myself and Trevor being detained for questioning. I'll go into more detail about those events later in the book but, predictably perhaps, the newspapers had a field day and it was a case of 'bad boy Ruddock in trouble again'. I maintained my innocence throughout, however, and that was borne out when the case came to court and I was acquitted of charges of 'threatening behaviour'. Me, threatening behaviour, how ridiculous! But that incident was typical of the sort of thing that gets blown out of all proportion when professional footballers are involved. Thank God I'm not as famous as Gazza.

It has certainly been an interesting couple of seasons at Upton Park what with the Hartson-Berkovic affair, the 1998 Christmas party, the signing of Paul Alcock's favourite player Paolo Di Canio, the Vieira spat, and the cup game involving Manny Omoyimni that had to be replayed. Like I said at the start of this chapter, there's never been a dull moment.

CHAPTER TWO

'Don't Mess With
The Ruddocks'

I was born in St George's Hospital, Tooting on 9 May
1968 – just a few weeks before Manchester United
became the first English team to win the European Cup
– and, apparently, Neil Ruddock was a trouble-maker
from the moment he made his first appearance. My
mum Joyce still likes to remind me how she had terrible
trouble giving birth to me, not to mention the fact that
I've been causing her grief ever since. I think she's half-
joking about the second bit, but the birth was definitely
no joke for her as I arrived prematurely and yet still
weighed in at over 10lb, so God knows what size I
would have been had mum gone the full term. The
doctors told her that I would have been a lot bigger if I
had received proper nutrition during the pregnancy. As
it was, there were all sorts of complications with the
birth and, as a result, the first few months of my life

were spent in hospital under the close watch of the staff.

It couldn't have been much fun for mum, who had set her heart on having a little girl, having already brought two big, bruising boys into the world, but we both came through the experience relatively unscathed. She was so convinced that child number three would be a girl that my parents had already decided on the name Hayley had I been born of the opposite gender. Thankfully, they settled on Neil and off we went to my first home at Mendip Crescent in Battersea. I can't remember anything about it as we moved to Ashford when I was still very young after the firm where my father Edward worked – Stewart Fraser, shop fitters – transferred their operation to Kent.

It must have been a bit of a culture shock for Mum and Dad as they had lived in the Wandsworth area of London all their lives. In fact they went to school together and, according to family legend, hated each other's guts as kids. But they found they had something in common when they became 'teddy boy and girl' during the Swinging Sixties and they've been rockin' and rollin' together ever since; as they still like to show us at weddings and family get-togethers.

As I got older I remember going back to London to visit family and friends but gradually they too moved away, with some living in Surrey and the rest in the same area of Kent where we had already set up home. At the time, Ashford was only a small village (until all our family arrived, that is!) but over the years it continued to expand and is quite a thriving town by local standards. In those days, though, we weren't particularly well off as a family. Dad worked hard – and so did mum as a cashier when all the kids were at school – to provide for us, and we never really wanted for anything. They always gave us what they could and one of my earliest presents, which I still possess to this day, was a plastic monkey called 'Jacko' who went everywhere with me and, as a result, that became my first ever nickname. My old friends from those early years still call me it to this day; 'Razor' didn't come until much, much later.

Apart from my monkey, material things weren't particularly important to me. As long as I had my football boots and a ball to kick around, I was happy. As we lived in Ashford – or 'Little London' as they called it when families like ours moved down and took over – and I was playing Sunday football in London and training there once a week, Dad would have to run me into town on a regular basis and that meant more to me than receiving presents, because I knew my parents struggled to find the money to get me to matches and to training all the time. If Dad hadn't been prepared to put himself out the way he did, it is unlikely I would ever have got the chance to make an impression in a decent league and, ultimately, make the grade as a professional. Where we lived in Kent, the standard of football wasn't so good and scouts never really ventured that far out of London, so I doubt I would ever have been spotted. Very few people did, and probably still do, make the grade from that part of the world.

My first school was called Willsborough and it became clear very early on in my education that soccer and not studying would be at the top of my priority list. School was about playing football, having a laugh and generally mucking around with my mates and the idea of getting a few qualifications under my belt wasn't something that appealed all that much. As I was a big lad as a kid, much bigger than others of my age, I always played with the older lads and could still hold my own in the playground if things got a bit tasty. Having two elder brothers, Gary and Colin (now 38 and 36 years old respectively) around meant that nobody would mess with us. Other lads soon realised that if they were going to pick on me and I wasn't in a position to defend myself, they would have my two brothers to contend with.

The bottom line was, if you mess with one Ruddock, you mess with them all.

In the end, they didn't bother and, as a result, I never really got into as many fights as I might have done had I been an only child. Because Gary and Colin were heavily into football, it was only natural for me to follow suit and, although I can't remember a specific time when I fell in love with the game, as they say, I just recall my early life being obsessed with it. Football, football, football; day-in, day-out. That was the way it was, which probably explains why I was never that good at school. It wasn't that I was thick or lacking in intelligence, I just wasn't interested in school, other than doing PE or playing football at break and lunchtimes. And then again as soon as we got home from school. We didn't have computer games, videos or the sort of extravagant playthings my children are fortunate to have nowadays, so it was a case of making your own entertainment (in most cases, playing football) or causing mayhem around the neigh-bourhood. I wasn't a particularly naughty kid but, like a lot of children, I got into the odd spot of bother. Nothing serious, just typically mischievous, childish pranks.

Sunday afternoons were always great fun because,

while our dads were either at home watching the *Big Match* on television or down the pub doing the same and enjoying the odd light ale in the process, we would be over the playing field acting out our own version of the *Big Match*. Then, when the pubs shut, as they did at about 3 o'clock in those days, all the half-cut fathers would come to the field to show off their skills. The fact that they'd had a few beers made them think they could turn back the clock to 'the good old days' when they were athletic kids with the same dreams we were harbouring. We used to laugh as they'd try all these fancy flicks, most of which never came off, and go running around the place boasting they were Kevin Keegan or Georgie Best. 'Watch this one, son!' would be a common shout from the old men as they attempted a 'Bobby Charlton rocket shot' or a curler into the top corner. Invariably the ball would go flying wide, or trickle pathetically towards goal but it was great to have the fathers out there, sharing our passion and love of the game; even though it usually required a few shandies to do the trick.

That was the norm in those days: loads of kids and their dads out in the park kicking balls about. You just don't see it so often these days and it's a shame because those Sunday afternoons before tea were special. Things you don't forget. My dad actually had a bit of a Bobby Charlton haircut, full sweep over, but in fairness he could actually play a bit. He had a wicked backheel on him; I remember that.

My brothers were seriously into their football and could probably have gone on to achieve something in the game because they were very good players, with all the attributes you look for in a young, potential pro: skill, pace, strength plus bundles of enthusiasm and confidence. But they discovered women and drink too early and that was the end of that. We all used to play for the same pub team, The Fox, and we certainly had some characters in the side; all nutters, but all great lads and decent footballers too. Every single one had a nickname which they are still known by today, and I can't let the opportunity pass without a full roll-call, so here goes...

Jacko (that was me), Phantom, Albert Hall, Dobber, Double Dobber (Dobber's big brother!), Bambi, Padge, Poker, Strutter, Legger, Remington, Roger Miller, Mad Mutley, Mental Meo, Doris Day, Hamstreet Village Hall, Spanner, Spud, Kid, Claud, Zubizaretta, Social, Lofty, Fagin, Striker, Woody, Willo, Homer, Oaksey, Bosko, Clark Kent, Snellars, Hodge, Spartacus, Ivan Lendl, Shergar, Judgement Day, Tonto, Ball Frog, W***** Williams, Shed, Dicky, Rossi, Bushy, Cone 'ead Matthews, Butch, Scotty Brooks, Yogi, Charlie the Limp, Tommo, Bert, Bullseye, Satellite's German Boyfriend, Chalky White, Tradesman's, Deno, Chilly, Signal Box, The Real Padgy, Fierce Lozza, Chief, Bunger, Silky, Meat and 2 Veg and Turkey Tel. Then there was Colin Wilton whose full title went something like ... *Colin Newton, with his suit on, works in distribution and lives in Walton and Newton.* Not forgetting ... *Ha, ha, ha, do excuse me, I didn't realise you played for Ashford Town, Storm the Bastille.* Apologies to those I've missed out.

As you can probably tell by that piece of self-indulgence, those days when life revolved around football and The Fox pub team were very special. I remember, for example, going along to watch my brothers play in a cup final for The Fox, a year or so before I'd made the team, and I was standing quite close to the touchline with my mum who loved to go along to games and cheer her boys on. At one point, the play switched to our end of the pitch and the linesman, eager to keep up with play, barged me out of the way and nearly knocked me to the ground. I was only 14 at the time and dear old mum wasn't going to stand for her 'little soldier' being pushed around. So the next time the 'lino' ventured past, mum gave him a right good kick and sent him flying! They had to stop the game and I think my brothers were dying with embarrassment out on the pitch. I guess that's where my fiery temperament comes from.

In fact, mum was sent off playing netball long before I'd seen my first red card. Myself and my two brothers went to watch her for the first time and when a player on the opposite side tripped her up, mum made a point of letting her opponent know she wasn't impressed. Her retaliation cost mum a year's ban!

So there wasn't much mum could say to my brother Colin not long after when he was playing in a big game by local standards, again for The Fox, and was at the centre of a fracas, shall we call it. As the trouble broke out, two players went for him, so he got his retaliation in first and knocked them both out. Needless to say, he was sent off and banned for a year as well. My other brother Gary also got banned for violent conduct at one point, but I never got into much trouble on the field during my younger days; all that came later. Although his temperament was a little suspect, Colin showed a lot of natural ability and could have gone on to greater things than the semi-pro circuit he ultimately settled for. But the team he played for wanted him to have his hair cut, go to bed early on a Friday night, all that sort of thing, and he wasn't having any of that. He allowed a career in football to pass him by, so when it came to my opportunity to make it he drummed it into me not to let it slip through my fingers.

'Don't make the same mistakes I did, and go for it', I remember Colin telling me. He could have achieved something in the game and he didn't want his little brother to make the same mistakes. He wouldn't let me get away with the sort of things he did and Mum and Dad warned me that I had a great chance and should take it. I was lucky because I learned from my brother's mistakes. I knew the pitfalls and I always had Colin there to turn to for advice. At the time I was playing for my Sunday team there were players in the side who were much better than me, but they went down the wrong path while I was fortunate and took the right route.

Obviously, I played for all my school teams as I was growing up and, because of my size, I was playing with the fourth years when I was a second-year junior. I was a confident lad who, because I was brought up playing with my brothers' friends who were that much older, was never intimidated playing against lads two, sometimes three years my senior. Perhaps that's what shaped me into the player I am today. I was uncompromising then because I had to be; it was a case of 'hit or be hit'. I quickly found out which one I preferred and you learn to look after yourself. I've been doing that ever since, although I'm the first to admit to going overboard from time to time. I don't consider myself a dirty player and I wasn't then. I can't remember getting booked that often as a kid and it wasn't until my England schoolboy days that I found out what it was like to be shown a red card.

I enjoyed playing for the school team and we had a fabulous sports teacher in Mr Jones who, I think, recognised the potential in me and encouraged me all the way. Bizarrely, he later became our milkman, not that such an earth-shattering revelation has any relevance to my story. But he was great, always keen to know how I'd got on at the weekend playing for Millwall youths, and generally instrumental in helping me take my first steps on the ladder towards becoming a professional footballer and, ideally, emulating my idol as a kid, Kevin Keegan.

Keegan was the main man in the 1970s and early 1980s and every kid on the park or in the school playground wanted to be him. Keegan was the George Best of his day, only with a clean-cut image, and he was the perfect role model for any kid. A bit like me nowadays! Mums loved him, dads admired him, girls drooled over him and boys idolised him and dreamed of achieving even a small percentage of what he achieved in the game. The first kit I ever had bought for me as a kid was a Liverpool strip, not because I supported them as a team, but purely and simply because of Keegan and the impact he made on me.

Thinking about it, even though the family was a little hard up, I used to do really well when it came to football kits. Because my birthday was on 9 May, just before the FA Cup final normally, I would get the strip of one of the two teams who'd reached Wembley as my birthday present. So, after getting a Liverpool kit in 1974 – when Keegan scored twice in the 3–0 win over Newcastle – I got a Fulham kit in 1975 when one of the legends of the game, Bobby Moore, captained the club in the twilight of his playing career. But the Liverpool one, because of

Keegan, was special. His attitude towards the game, like Bobby Moore himself, was spot on and it's no surprise that he has gone on to acquire the ultimate job as manager of his country. Apart from Terry Venables, I can't think of a better man for the position of England coach and I'm sure he'll be as successful as an international manager as he was an England footballer.

While Keegan was my 'national hero' if you like, closer to home my idols were Millwall players, obviously, with John Mitchell – who later went on to play for Fulham – arguably my favourite. Other players at the club I admired were people like Anton Otulakowski, big Dave Cusack and, a little bit later, Teddy Sheringham who was only a couple of years older than me but someone I looked up to and loved watching.

Another hero of mine when I first started going to watch football was Chelsea's Tommy Langley who actually scored in a 3–1 win over Liverpool at Stamford Bridge in the FA Cup in the first professional game I ever went to see in 1978. I was even more smitten by the idea of becoming a pro-footballer from then on.

Whilst living down in Ashford, I became very close to a family called the Tworts who moved back to London where one of the boys, Mark, went on to sign apprenticeship forms for Millwall. Envious, or what? A while later I was playing for Ashford in the Kent Cup final and our opposition on the day was South London, and Mark was playing for them. We beat them in the final and afterwards Mark encouraged me to come up to London to play for his Sunday team, St Thomas More. And that was the turning point really, because within months of playing for them I was picked up by Millwall, so I have a lot to thank Mark for. If I'd carried on playing out in the sticks of Kent, I doubt I would have been spotted. The scouts didn't seem to venture that far and the chances of players making it from that part of the world were remote to say the least. So I was on the way to playing for the team I supported as a boy and couldn't have been happier. Not that it was the case for all the family. Half of them supported Millwall, the other half Fulham, but there was never any doubt where my allegiance would lie even though my dad was Fulham through and through and would have loved me to play for them if I ever made it as a pro. I'm afraid there was never any danger of that happening and there was only one team I wanted to play for – the Lions of Millwall. My brothers and all my cousins, whom I loved and looked up to, supported Millwall and I followed suit because it was more fashionable as a young lad to follow the Lions. *'No-one likes us; we don't care'* and all that. It was that sort of era. Millwall fans had a reputation for being nutters in those days and trouble was never very far away. Not that we would dream of starting it!

The worst and most notorious occasion happened in March 1985 (I was 16) when thousands of Millwall fans went on the rampage at Luton's tiny Kenilworth Road ground during an FA Cup quarter-final tie. People, from the FA big-wigs up to then Prime Minister Margaret Thatcher, called it the worst case of football hooliganism in the history of the British game and I suppose, even though I had a vested interest, they were right. To coin a London phrase, 'it all kicked off, big time'. Seats were being ripped out and thrown onto the pitch and then there was a full-scale battle with police on the field itself with the supporters grabbing what they could – bits of wood, broken up hoardings, anything – to use as weapons or to throw at the boys in blue. It was scary stuff and I was right there in the middle of it. Not that I was involved in any acts of violence, you understand. I was trying to get out of the way.

But there was no denying my presence on the Kenilworth Road pitch because the next day there was my big, ugly mug plastered all over the back page of the *South London Press*, under the banner headline of 'THUGS!', right at the centre of all the chaos. Not the sort of impression I was looking to make as a first year apprentice at The Den! I can't remember what caused it all to kick off – I don't think the Millwall fans behind one of the goals took too kindly to the fact that bricks were being thrown into the away end – but it didn't usually take much. There were a lot of people injured and the stadium was wrecked, as were a number of shops, houses and cars outside the ground; not to mention the train which eventually took the Millwall supporters who didn't get arrested back to London. It was all shown on television and to the watching nation it was a night of shame, but to the majority of the fans involved it was a triumph against authority; a throwback to the days of the mods and rockers having running battles with the law down in Brighton.

Even though the image of the sport, along with that of Millwall Football Club, had been seriously damaged, as far as the fans were concerned it added to their reputation as the biggest and baddest set of supporters in the country. They were notorious and proud of it. The old Den, as any visiting player or fan would tell you, was an intimidating place to go to and the entrance via the underpass at the Cold Blow Lane End wasn't the most welcoming sight in the world. But we loved it and the fact that we knew other teams hated coming there made it even better. They just wanted to get those 90 minutes of hell out of the way and get out of there.

Things aren't the same now. The New Den, as good a stadium as it is, is just too nice and I think Millwall as a team have suffered as a result of the atmosphere being not as hostile, and visiting players actually enjoy playing there.

Anyway, back to that infamous riot at Luton. It wasn't until the day after when I saw all the papers and the news on television that the enormity of it all began to register. And it wasn't until I saw the following day's edition of the *South London Press* that I realised how much trouble I had got myself into. After all, I was a Millwall apprentice and George Graham was my manager. Of course, I denied any involvement and maintained that while the picture looked bad, I was actually running away from the trouble and any potential confrontation with the police because I realised that, even as a young player at Millwall, I was still 'a representative of the club'. I thought that line might go down well, and George seemed to accept my version of events and little more was said of the matter, but I was a bit worried about getting a reputation as a trouble-maker so soon after I'd achieved my life-long ambition of being signed up as a junior for the club of my dreams.

As I said earlier, I was never bothered about my education and couldn't wait to get out of school each day, get home and play more football. When it came to the fifth year I only went into school twice a week and the rest of the time I was doing work experience down at Millwall, which was great. I'd known for a while that I was going to become a footballer and didn't see that there was any point in studying any further; not that I did much beforehand. It was through my Sunday team, St Thomas More, that I got my break with Millwall because most of the lads I played with were on the club's books and it seemed a natural progression for me to follow them. That's exactly what happened, and in my final year at school I was training down the Den three times a week. I'd signed schoolboy forms at the age of 14 with a two-year apprenticeship, so when I left school I knew I had a job lined up and school meant nothing. Of course, as a father you don't say that to your own kids because education now is so important and I would never underestimate that. But in those days it was different.

I wouldn't allow my kids to do what I did. My son Josh is eight years old and all he wants to do is play football, football, football – just like me at his age. But just as my dad never pushed me, I would never do that to my boy. I'll wait until he's old enough to decide for himself – then tell him he can't do it! When I was playing for St Thomas More, loads of dads used to come down shouting and screaming at their boys and getting on their backs, but my dad would never do that and I wouldn't allow myself to put pressure on Josh by doing it. If those lads had a bad game, their dads would be right on their backs but my old man, whenever he came to watch, would never say I was crap or I'd had a good game, he just left me to get on with my own football. Even at that age you know whether you've played well or badly. You don't need your father jumping down your throat every five minutes.

We had a very successful team at St Thomas More, and during my time there we won the London Cup three years running which was quite an achievement. Playing in a good side brought the best out of me and must have persuaded Millwall that I had a fair chance of making the grade as a pro. What I didn't realise at the time was that I'd make my mark as a central defender because, as a kid, I always played up front. George Graham was the man who signed me on schoolboy forms and when I first started training with Millwall, my first coach was a guy called Roger Cross and, strangely enough, he's my coach now at West Ham. I'd play Saturdays for Millwall boys and sometimes turn out for the reserves in midweek whilst still playing on Sundays for St Thomas More with virtually the same set of players. While I was playing for the Millwall youth team, I remember coming up against the likes of Tony Adams at Arsenal, Paul Ince at West Ham, Tim Sherwood at Watford, Alan Shearer and Matt Le Tissier for Southampton and a number of the Spurs lads I was later to play alongside: characters like John Moncur, David Howells and Vinny Samways.

The good thing about Millwall was the fact that I could play youth team football against players like that and then step up a level to play for the reserves, which would never have happened at a bigger club. It was great experience, because you'd be coming up against senior pros coming back from injury or reaching the tail end of their careers and it was good to measure yourself, in terms of ability and temperament, against players of this quality. It certainly stood me in good stead.

In my last year at school, all I could think about was getting away and working full-time at Millwall. I was training there three days a week as it was and, in the end, I only took one exam because I simply hadn't studied. I just sat CSE Art and got a grade two and that was all I had to show for it. But I was taking up the career I had always wanted and I can't imagine that too many of the lads I went to school with can say that. There was certainly no-one from my school who went into football, mainly because it wasn't a big soccer area. I guess that's one of the reasons why my headmaster, Mr Coulson I seem to remember his name was, didn't think I was very wise to throw away my chance of a decent education for the sake of taking up such an uncertain career. He obviously didn't rate my chances of becoming a successful sports-man too highly, because I recall him saying to me one day, 'Ruddock, you will not make it as a professional footballer as long as you've got a hole in your a***!' So much for his assessment of my career potential. If you're reading this, Mr Coulson…

CHAPTER THREE

George Graham –
My First Agent

It was the summer of 1985 and I had just begun my two-year apprenticeship at Millwall when my father landed a five-year contract to work in Saudi Arabia and decided to move out there with Mum. Obviously, I was sorry to see them go, but joining them was never a consideration. Nothing was going to divert me from the route I'd mapped out, or had been mapped out for me. My parents under-stood and, while I hoped at least they were going to miss me, they were confident their 'little boy' would be okay going out into the big, wide world alone. I was probably a bit more mature (maybe 'streetwise' would be a better description) than most teenagers and I always had my brothers, cousins and friends to turn to in times of trouble.

So, when I was 16, I left home and moved into digs with the parents of Roger Cross, one of the Millwall coaches, out in Barking. Roger was brilliant to me, although he certainly didn't allow me to take liberties just because my parents were thousands of miles away, and he used to keep me in order. As best he could, that is. I can't speak highly enough of Roger – and the other people on the staff at Millwall – because they did so much for me in those early days when I could, quite easily, have gone right off the rails and blown my career virtually before it had begun. I'll never forget how Roger and his family took me under their wing while my parents were out of the country and a lot of the success I've enjoyed in my career is down to the guidance and support they gave me at that time.

I was such a confident lad, cocky some might say, that I wasn't unduly worried about leaving home at such an early age, with Mum and Dad no longer around for support, because if that's what it took to follow my chosen career path, then so be it. I knew I would cope. I would see my parents every few months when dad came back on leave, but my brothers were always there for me and I'd stay with them on occasions so it wasn't a problem. I lived with the Crosses in Barking for two years and throughout that time they also provided a home for a lad called Gary Middleton, a Geordie, who was living away from his family like me, and we became good mates. He was in the same boat and we were like brothers. If I had been on my own it might have been difficult but, knowing he was going through the same sort of thing, it was okay and we shared a lot of experiences as teenagers becoming adults.

I never doubted that I would make it as a pro, even though there were no guarantees just because I'd got a two-year apprenticeship. But what was a surprise was the position I ended up playing because, as a kid, I was always a left winger or a centre-forward with a cunning eye for goal (hear that, Wrighty?). I was signed up by Millwall originally as a striker because I was a big lad who scored plenty of goals and that's what I thought I would be doing from then on. Like most kids, I dreamed of scoring goals for my favourite team, hitting the winner at Wembley and all that kind of *Boy's Own* stuff. That was still my dream when I joined Millwall and when I was playing for the youth team in the South-East Counties League, while I was still in my fifth year at school.

I was playing against 18-year-olds when I was 15 and still holding my own, so it was a great experience which stood me in good stead for when I turned pro and was playing against 'real' men. Hard men, too. My physical presence, coupled with the ability I had, meant I was a real handful even at that stage of my development. Too much of a handful, as far as former Liverpool and Scotland striker Ian St John was concerned, when he brought a team of foreigners over to play our youth team at the Crystal Palace athletics stadium one year. St John, who ran his own coaching camp, was taking his team around different clubs and introducing them to the finer points of English football … so coming to Millwall was a big mistake! They were all big lads, a year older than us, so when they started putting themselves about I decided it was time for them to taste some of their own medicine. But St John didn't like it when I started laying into some of his boys and he was going mad on the touchline, calling me all the names under the sun and almost getting into a fight with coaches Roger Cross and Bob Pearson in the process. But that was the way we were brought up at Millwall. If the opposition started something, we were more than happy to finish it. St John wasn't happy with me and, in hindsight, those incidents might possibly have had something to do with him giving me a load of stick some years later when I was playing for Liverpool and he was a television and radio pundit.

It wasn't until my first year as an apprentice when we were playing in a friendly at Gravesend that I came to be acquainted with defensive duties. Our team was short of players at the back and Theo Foley, who was then assistant manager to George Graham, said to me, 'How do you fancy playing at centre-half?' Although I'd never played there before, I said I would give it a go. I performed pretty well in that game, was powerful in the air, snuffed out their centre-forward without too much trouble and, as I was used to playing further up the field, was able to knock it about a bit at the back too. The management were obviously impressed with my debut in that position because I stayed there and never played centre-forward again, other than on a couple of occasions in an emergency. Mind you, it didn't stop me scoring goals and in my last year in the youth team I scored 26 goals … from centre-half! About half of them were from penalties, I admit, but the rest were either bullet headers from corners or stunning free-kicks from 25 yards. Honest! Either way, not a bad goalscoring effort for a defender. Roger Cross still talks about it today.

My dream of being the goal hero at Wembley may have gone, but that sudden switch was to re-shape the whole course of my career. Who knows, had I stayed at centre-forward I may not have made the grade and it's a fair bet I wouldn't have enjoyed as much fame, fortune and success that I have as a defender. I would probably have been a Joe Jordan-type striker (only better looking!) but ended up marking players of his kind instead. And I've loved every minute of it, quite frankly. As people might have gathered by now, I do enjoy the physical side of the game and, being a big lad capable of looking after himself, I've never shied away from a challenge. It doesn't matter how big or tough they are, or think they are. They don't come much harder than my old Millwall colleague John Fashanu, but I never had any trouble with him. I certainly never feared him, despite his reputation. And I think that he respected me because whenever I played against him, I never backed off or ducked a tackle. Show the Fash fear and you're dead.

So perhaps I was destined to be a stopper rather than a scorer and, having had the benefit of playing up front, I was aware of what strikers were thinking about, the sort of runs they would make and when they were likely to strike at goal. I suppose it was as a result of me switching positions that I developed the hard man tag, because suddenly I was a defender and I would do my best to stop strikers at all cost, which often meant a booking or a sending off, something I've certainly not been a stranger to over the years.

It was a brush with officialdom, however, which I feared was going to cost me dearly as a Millwall apprentice on the verge of earning myself a professional contract. While I avoided any real hassle over the Kenilworth Road affair, I wasn't so lucky some time after when me and Gary Middleton, the lad whom I shared digs with in Barking, were involved in an incident outside a Pizza Hut in Pimlico one evening. It was nothing more than a 'handbags' confrontation with another couple of lads which resulted in the police being called. We weren't charged with anything, but George Graham managed to find out and the next morning we were summoned to the boss's office and I have never been so scared in my life. Even in those days, before he had really made his mark as a manager, George was recognised for his strict policy on discipline and I feared the worst as we went to see him and explain our actions.

Having made a good impression in both the youth team and the reserves, I was already knocking on the door of the first team at the time and should have been keeping my nose clean and putting pressure on the manager to give me a chance in the senior side, not giving him the opportunity to kick me out of the club. But, boys will be boys, and Gary and myself were definitely stupid boys on this occasion. All sorts of questions and doubts were racing through my mind as we prepared to face the wrath of George: 'What is he going to say ... will he kick us out ... what am I going to tell Mum and Dad when they next come back from Saudi?' All these thoughts and more were tossing about inside my head and, big and brave as I was or thought I was, I was scared. The potential consequences didn't bear thinking about.

Sheepishly, we approached his office and after youth coach Roger Cross had been in to tell George what had happened, it was our turn. He seemed very calm as we walked in and he was sat behind his desk, but we didn't expect a sympathetic hearing and, sure enough, we didn't get one. He went absolutely ballistic. He told us we had let ourselves down, let our families down and, perhaps more importantly, let the club down and he was determined to teach us a lesson we wouldn't forget. Thankfully, he didn't kick us out as we'd feared, but he did put us on ground duty from 9 am to 5 pm, three days a week for two weeks: doing odd jobs around the stadium, cleaning and painting The Den hour after hour. It was his way of showing us what sort of jobs we could end up doing if we continued to jeopardise our careers in football. It was a real eye-opener, I can tell you, and the whole episode had a profound effect on me; my head went down and I was absolutely gutted for days afterwards.

But then, completely out of the blue, I got the pick-me-up I badly needed when George selected me to play in a Freight Rover Trophy game at Southend, my first-team debut for the club. I wasn't sure if he was playing mind games with me or not, but having told me on the Saturday night I would be playing on the Wednesday, sure enough he picked me. I did alright and we won 2–0 and that was my introduction to first-team football. But then, having been on a high after making my first-team debut, I was back in at 9 o'clock the next morning doing jobs around the ground, painting this and that, and I reckon that was George's way of bringing me back down to earth and letting me know that he hadn't forgotten what had happened a week or so before.

That wasn't the only time George put me on ground duty, cleaning the terraces, because that was also my punishment when I upset him by going to the toilet up against a fence at the training ground, rather than walking the 100 yards or so back to the dressing rooms. In his eyes I was showing a lack of discipline, a lack of respect if you like, and he was determined to let me know that sort of behaviour was unacceptable at his club; especially when he was around. But that was typical of him and his attitude towards our profession, even in those early days. Although he was the first-team manager, he took a great interest in the youth teams, mainly because he didn't have money to spend on players from other clubs and he was dependent on youngsters coming up through the ranks. He set high standards and was always pulling the young lads up for having dirty kit or dirty boots, and he certainly knew how to get the message across. As I had now found out to my cost on a couple of occasions.

I thought the punishment for just peeing up against a fence was a bit harsh, but I couldn't argue with the way he handled my other transgression. Looking back, I think it was good management by George because he was letting me see both ends of the footballing spectrum and giving me the chance to decide which road I wanted to go down. Having sampled life in the first team, he was letting me know what I could be missing out on if I allowed myself to keep getting into trouble and be a Big-Time Charlie. He really knocked that home to me and taught me a lesson. It was his way of letting me know that I could blow the chance of a lifetime and he certainly made sure his message was received and understood. It did have a positive affect on me at the time and certainly made me think. You hear of a lot of youngsters, many with more ability than I'll ever have, throwing it all away because they go off the rails, and I was damned sure that wasn't going to happen to me. I'll always be grateful to George for that, amongst other things. He gave me my debut at a time when I didn't deserve it because I'd been so stupid and, by giving me a taste of first-team life, I wanted more of it, no doubt about that.

I'd made my reserve team debut at the age of 16, against West Ham strangely enough, towards the end of the 1983–84 season and it was early the following season when I took my senior bow in the Freight Rover game against Southend at Roots Hall. Not the most glamorous of settings for your introduction to first-team life, but I didn't care where it was or who we were playing – especially after everything that had gone on before. It wasn't the best of games either and, although we won 2–0 with me setting up one of the goals for skipper Alan McLeary, the match was best remembered for a free-for-all involving about a dozen players (not me, I hasten to add). The local paper described it as 'an ugly melee with fists and boots flying' and I can recall one of their players, Tony Hadley, being taken to hospital with a broken jaw. Ironically, it had all kicked off as a result of a late tackle by Warren May on me, so I was the innocent party for a change.

I didn't play a league game for Millwall in that first spell and only managed another three more Freight Rover appearances because we got knocked out of the competition. During that 1984–85 season, I played in a first-team friendly against a Spurs side that contained the likes of Glenn Hoddle and Garth Crooks who, if memory serves me correctly, were coming back from injuries at the time. I don't recall much about the game, but I do remember going over to White Hart Lane, seeing the set-up and the calibre of players they had there and thinking that, one day, I would love to play for a big, glamorous club like Spurs. Little did I know that before the season was through, I would actually be signing on the dotted line for the North London giants. At the time we played them, however, nothing could have been further from my mind. I hadn't even played a league game for Millwall and I was only 17, so there was no rush. I'd only recently signed professional terms for the Lions anyway.

For the time being, I was content with playing in the reserves and concentrating on doing well at that level because you were always aware that scouts and coaches from other clubs, not just your own management team, were out there running the rule over potential stars whom they might be able to pick up for a relatively small fee. That must be how Spurs initially took an interest in me.

The first I knew of any approach from White Hart Lane was one morning when, as I reported for training, I got a message from Roger Cross that the gaffer wanted to see me in his office. I remember thinking, 'Oh no, not again – what have I done now?' Normally, the only time you went to see George in his office was when you were in trouble, as I was only too well aware. So somewhat nervously, and not having a clue what this 'little chat' was going to be about, I showed up about 10.30 on the morning of what I was soon to realise was transfer deadline day, although I wasn't aware of it at the time. I walked in, shuffled in more like, and straightaway the boss told me that he had sold John Fashanu to Wimbledon for what was then a club record £120,000. I wondered what Fash's departure had to do with me, unless George wanted to switch me back up front to the now vacant centre-forward role. So you can imagine my surprise when he went on to say that he had received two offers for me, one from Norwich and the other from Spurs.

I was stunned to the core. George said that he didn't want to sell me, but the money was good and, considering Millwall's financial plight at the time, he was obliged to take the offers seriously. The decision, at the end of the day, was mine because I was under contract. George said that I'd got half an hour to make my mind up. Half an hour to make the biggest decision of my life, and with my parents halfway across the world. Because everything had happened so suddenly, I didn't have time to take it all in; it was exciting, yet frightening, all at the same time. My mind was racing and I couldn't think straight.

George said he had spoken to my father on the phone in Saudi to tell him what was going on and the message from Dad was that it was up to me. Great, thanks Dad! I went away to weigh up my options and George followed me, saying, 'Look son, you can go to Norwich and be in their first team in three months or you can go to Spurs and prove yourself in the reserves over the next year or two'. The idea of first-team football in Division One appealed, but I couldn't get excited about joining Norwich, no offence But Spurs were a big club, a massive club in fact, with players like Glenn Hoddle, Ossie Ardiles, Chrissy Waddle and Clive Allen. And I was only a 17-year-old boy. It was a big decision for a kid, even a confident lump like me, especially as I didn't have time to turn to my parents, nor even my brothers, for advice or guidance. It was make your mind up time, *now*. And it was all down to me. The thing I do remember most about what George was saying, and a lot of it was going in one ear and out of the other with all the excitement (*fear, more like*), was 'a lot of people go and watch Tottenham reserves play, so if you don't make it into the first team you've always got a good chance of getting a move elsewhere'. Sounded reasonable enough. But my head was still spinning.

In the end I decided on taking a chance with Spurs and George did the rest. I don't think he wanted to get rid of me because of the Pizza Hut incident, but he did seem very keen on me getting over to White Hart Lane as quickly as possible. So much so that he drove me up to North London himself before negotiating my personal terms for me with Tottenham boss Peter Shreeve. George Graham – my very first agent!

Obviously, I was very nervous going into the meeting with Mr Shreeve, even though George had done his best to put my mind at rest with words of reassurance during the journey up from South London. I don't know how I would have handled the situation if he had not been with me, but he took care of everything. Once we were in the manager's office, it was all about George and all I had to do was nod in agreement every now and then. The transfer fee was £70,000 down, with another £230,000 depending on appearances, which was quite a lot for a 17-year-old kid who had never played league football before. Obviously they saw the raw potential! At the time I had just turned pro and was earning £150 a week and after dishing out the customary speil about what a great club I would be joining, and what opportunities it would present, they offered me £225 a week, which I thought was great. A £75 a week pay rise which, to me at the time, was big bucks. Lovely. But suddenly George jumped up out of his seat and blurted out, '£225 a week? You mean to say I've brought this kid all the way here for a paltry £225 a week?' and with that he started to walk out of the room, dragging me with him on the way. By now I was totally bemused by the whole thing. 'Come on lad, we're going,' George said to me and with that I thought the deal was off. But as we were on the way out,

George winked at me as if to say, 'It's alright son, I'll sort you out', and we marched off. As we walked down the corridor Peter Shreeve came running out of his office screaming. 'George, George, don't be like that, come back! Let's talk.' So with that we went back into the office and they ended up giving me about £350 a week and a Ford Escort XR3. And I couldn't even drive!

Needless to say, I was delighted with the deal and had no hesitation in putting pen to paper for one of the most glamorous clubs in the country. I just couldn't believe my luck and I walked away from White Hart Lane with my head in the clouds thinking, 'That's it, I've made it'. Even to this day, whenever I see George, I always thank him for what he did for me. He was my first agent, and he didn't cost me a penny. He looked after me at a time when my parents were thousands of miles away and their 'little boy' was making the biggest move of my life. George was great: during that period he was my dad, my agent, my advisor. He did everything for me and I won't forget that. Every time I see him he always asks after my mum and dad and I will always have the highest regard for him. To think, a few months before he had hauled me over the coals and put me on ground duty for being a naughty boy; the next he was putting me on the road to stardom and setting me up financially for life. Cheers, George!

CHAPTER FOUR

Winning My Spurs – and My First England Caps

My move to Tottenham capped a whirlwind month when everything seemed to be happening at once. While I was still a Millwall player I was selected to play for the England youth side against the Republic of Ireland at Elland Road and I can still remember how chuffed I was when George Graham broke the news to me. I was even more proud when I realised that my dad had flown all the way back from Saudi to witness my international debut at the home of Leeds United on 25 February 1986. Obviously I had phoned him and Mum to tell them about getting an England call-up, but I had no idea that he was planning to come home and share my big day. I must have done alright in the game because soon afterwards I was named in the England squad for the Under-18 European Youth Championship clash with

Scotland, a game which took place at Aberdeen's Pittodrie ground just three days before my surprise transfer to Spurs. We got hammered by the Scots that day, but I wasn't down for too long as 'my dream move' wiped away the disappointment as I looked forward to a new phase in my life.

Obviously, going to a big club at such a young age was very exciting, but it was also a bit scary because the standard of players at White Hart Lane was that much higher and I wondered if I would be out of my depth. I needn't have worried too much, and some comments from Peter Shreeve's assistant at the time, John Pratt, gave me a lot of confidence in the early days. He was quoted in the press as saying: 'We have been looking at Neil for some time and he's impressed on each occasion. I'm sure he's a good investment.' Things like that do wonders for your confidence and, although I didn't play a first-team game for Spurs during the remainder of the 1985–86 season, I was pleased with the progress I was making in the youth and reserve sides. How can you not progress, and not learn, when you're training every day with the likes of Glenn Hoddle and Ossie Ardiles? That alone was an inspiration and when I thought about what they had achieved in the game, it made me even more determined to try and follow in their footsteps. Even in the short space of time I'd been at White Hart Lane, I was developing as a player and already harbouring hopes and ambitions of playing alongside my idols in the first team, not just chasing after them on the training pitch. Like I said, I was pleased with the progress I was making and I think the management were as well.

I was doing okay on the international front too, as I was named in the England youth squad for a three-match, 18-day tour of China; my first real footballing trip abroad. I'd only ever been to Leyton Orient, but now I was going to the real thing! Having made a few appearances for my country earlier in the year, I had half expected to be named in the squad, but it was still a great thrill – and an honour – when the club received confirmation that I was in the 17-man party for a tournament in Peking. The great thing about it was that I wasn't the only player from Spurs making the trip, as both David Howells and Vinny Samways had been called up as well. There were a number of other quality players in the squad who also went on to make excellent careers for themselves, people like Michael Thomas (Arsenal), Tony Daley (Aston Villa), David Hirst (Barnsley) and Kevin Pressman (Sheffield Wednesday).

The prospect of playing against Brazil, France and the host nation China (we even played the Korean army at one stage) was an exciting one and I was as proud as anything as I boarded the plane with the rest of the lads, all kitted out in our England blazers complete with the three lions. The light blue jackets perhaps weren't the height of fashion at the time, but that didn't matter because we had been selected to represent our country in a foreign land; the cream of the crop, so to speak. I've still got the blazer tucked away in a cupboard somewhere and it still makes me smile, with pride as much as anything else, when I take it out to look at it from time to time.

Not only was it a great privilege to be part of an England squad on tour, it was fantastic to have the opportunity to visit the sort of places you would never have dreamed of going to. It was hardly Southend-on-Sea! What's more, we were treated like kings wherever we went; everything was laid on for us. Even more amazing was the fact that we played in front of 100,000 people against China in the national stadium, an incredible experience for a group of lads more used to crowds of 2–3,000 in our respective reserve sides. I've never seen so many bicycles in one place; there must have been 99,000 all lined up around the stadium! We managed to reach the final and although we lost 2–1 to Brazil we hadn't disgraced ourselves and the disappointment of that was massively outweighed by the fact that we'd had the time of our lives. In addition to the football, we visited all the sights and walking along the Great Wall of China was something special. It was also a decent workout because there were about 3,000 steps leading up to it – we didn't need to train after that!

One of the amusing things was when we played against China, because all their players were about a foot smaller than me! But while we were physically stronger than them, they were very quick, very fit and it was a good test playing against such a different form of opposition. It was the same with the Brazilians – even at such a young age, their technique and skill on the ball was amazing. It was something we could all learn from. To top the trip off, the Football Association took the whole squad to Hong Kong for three days, which was something else to crow about to my mates when we returned home – as well as showing off all the dodgy Lacoste T-shirts and fake Rolex watches I'd bought for about a quid. None of the lads knew what a Rolex was, so I went to a jewellers to get a brochure and pointed out that the watch I was wearing, a gift from the Chinese Ambassador I boasted, was worth £6,000. They were gutted.

When I reported back for pre-season training at Spurs, I wondered how long I would have to wait for a taste of first-team football and the answer was ... not long. I was picked to play in what was supposed to be a 'friendly' against Glasgow Rangers, a testimonial match for Tottenham's long-serving defender Paul Miller. The match was anything but friendly and, as it was the first time Rangers had been allowed to play in London for 16 years after previous incidents of violence in the capital, the occasion had a real edge to it. The kick-off was delayed by 15 minutes as a wall of police marched thousands of Rangers' fans back to their part of the ground after they had tried to encroach into the Tottenham end. The fact that Graeme Souness had just taken over at Ibrox and had made a string of English players – people like Chris Woods and Terry Butcher – his first signings, added a bit more spice to the occasion. Yours truly didn't exactly help matters by clattering into Iain Ferguson early on with a full-blooded challenge which led to my first introduction to that fiery Scot Souness, who was later to become my boss at Liverpool.

The Rangers' boss, still a player-manager at the time, was the first on the scene after seeing one of his players flattened by this young upstart. He grabbed me by the throat and, with a few choice expletives, left me in no doubt what he thought of my challenge. I can't recall his exact words, although they were obviously not too complimentary, but I do remember thinking his reactions were a bit out of order, especially as he was no stranger to putting his foot in himself. I called him a bully, or something similar, as I was only a 'baby' at the time. A few years later when I signed for him at Anfield, my mind went back to that incident and I said to him, 'I bet you wouldn't square up to me now' and he assured me that he would! I always had respect for Souness, both as a player and a manager, and during my teenage years he was something of an idol of mine because of the way he approached the game. I loved the fact that a player with so much skill and ability was totally committed and never found wanting when the going got tough. Some of his tackles, those two-footed studs-up affairs, were pretty scary but he was a winner through and through and the sort of player you would want on your side.

It was around the time of Paul Miller's testimonial, which earned him around £50,000 I seem to remember, that the club held its customary, start-of-season photocall and I turned up expecting to be in the reserve team line-up which was also being photographed that day. As the snappers were setting up their shots David Pleat, who had taken over as manager from Peter Shreeve in the summer of 1986, suddenly called me over and told me to line-up with the first-team squad. That was a proud moment for me as it suggested a break-through into the senior side was on the cards. The other lads in the reserves, especially John Moncur, were absolutely gutted and I took a lot of stick over that. Not that I minded. I've still got the picture and I looked as proud as punch as I took my place between Paul Miller and Ray Clemence, with the likes of such international superstars as Hoddle and Ardiles just in front of me.

As I'd been away on tour with the England youth squad, I didn't know too much about the managerial merry-go-round going on back at White Hart Lane. When I left for China, Peter Shreeve was the manager; when I returned for pre-season training, David Pleat was in charge. I was pretty surprised because we hadn't had that bad a season and no-one thought that Shreevesy, and his assistant John Pratt, were under too much pressure. As Peter was the man who'd signed me, with a helping hand from George Graham, I was sad to see him go because he was a nice bloke and a good boss in my view. Plus, from a purely personal point of view, a new manager coming in invariably wants to sign his own players and that puts pressure on those already at the club; especially those who had only recently been signed by the outgoing manager. Because I'd not had the opportunity to make an impression in the first team, I wondered whether the new boss would fancy me, or whether he would show me the door. From the club's point of view, however, it was seen as an excellent coup because Pleat arrived with an impressive CV and a top-drawer reputation after doing such a magnificent job at Luton. The general thinking was that if he can create a successful team from next-to-nothing, what could he achieve, given a few quid to spend? Tottenham were moving on to bigger and better things, so the powers that be predicted, and it was reassuring to know that Pleat felt I had a part to play in those plans. As well as putting me in the first team photo, he told me as much before the season started. He understood that I was 'a bit raw', but he said that with the right application and determination I could have a bright future at the club. And he also assured me that, although I'd only been at White Hart Lane a short time and was a 'Shreeve signing', he had an open mind about me as a player and a person. I would get a chance to impress as much as the next man and it was what I did from then on that mattered, which came as a great boost. In fact, I was on top of the world during pre-season.

But while I made it onto the team photo and was given a shot in the arm by Pleat's comments, I didn't get a look-in as far as first-team action went until the last couple of months of the season, with Spurs still in the hunt for a League and Cup double. We were sitting pretty in third place in the old First Division and were in the quarter-finals of the FA Cup and, with Clive Allen scoring goals for fun that 1986–87 season, there was every chance we would end up with a trophy, or two. Even though he was playing up front on his own virtually from day one, Clive was on fire and he broke Jimmy Greaves' scoring record of 44 goals before going on to end the season just one short of the 50 mark in all competitions. Mind you, he did have Glenn Hoddle and Chris Waddle pulling the strings behind him and creating an endless supply of chances, most of which he put away that season.

'Widdly' Waddle, in particular, was outstanding that season and was an absolute delight to watch. He was also a pleasure to work with on the training ground and took a great interest in the younger players like myself, always having the time to talk to us and pass on the benefit of his experience. I remember being so impressed with his professionalism, and loved him for it from then on. He was a great favourite with everyone at White Hart Lane and it's a shame that, like Hoddle, he perhaps never got the recognition in this country that his unbelievable skills deserved.

It wasn't really until they took their talents abroad – Glenn to Monaco and Chris to Marseille – that they were fully appreciated. Not that it was ever in doubt amongst the staff at Spurs. Just watching them in action on the training pitch was a treat in itself, although trying to mark Chris was an absolute nightmare because he had so many tricks and skills in his locker. When I used to come up against him, I often knew, or thought I knew, what he was going to do to try and beat me, but there was still nothing I could do about it. I'd still end up sitting on my backside or facing the wrong way after he'd turned me inside out a few times. I can recall him playing against Kenny Wharton and leaving the Newcastle defender on the seat of his pants, jinking one way and then the other before going past him without actually touching the ball. A magnificent player and someone we could all learn so much from. I remember thinking at the time that, when I got older, I would be like Waddle and take time to help the kids. I'd like to think that's what I've done wherever I've played. Of course, I could never dream of possessing the sort of skills Chris, and Glenn had, but I know what their words of encouragement and advice meant to me at that time and I've never forgotten them.

My big moment, my first senior appearance in a competitive match, came in the FA Cup quarter-final clash with Wimbledon on 15 March 1987. I'd made the bench a few times already and was one of the subs for the visit to Plough Lane which everyone had said we wouldn't fancy one little bit. We knew what to expect from Wimbledon – with people like Vinnie Jones and John Fashanu in the side it was always going to be a battle – but the lads were up for it that day and the backline, Gary Mabbutt in particular, was magnificent. After weathering the early storm, Chris Waddle put us in the lead midway through the second half and that was my signal to get ready for battle and I came on as a replacement for Ossie Ardiles with the instructions to keep things tight at the back, and preserve that lead at all costs. We did better than that.

Within five minutes of coming on, we were awarded a free-kick about 30 yards out and I can remember hearing David Pleat shout from the bench 'Ruddock shoot, Ruddock shoot!' I was flattered by his confidence in me and was more than happy to oblige until the master, Glenn Hoddle, took control of proceedings, grabbing the ball and politely pushing me to one side, saying, 'Stand back, son, leave this to me'. I was hardly in a position to argue so up stepped Glenn and, with one wonderful strike, he put us 2–0 up and on course for Wembley. It was an incredible moment and as Glenn ran off to take the acclaim of the fans, I went after him and I was the first to jump on his back as everyone went absolutely mental. The pictures in the papers the next day were of an ecstatic Hoddle with this big lump on his back going mad. What an introduction.

Sadly, I didn't make the team for the semi-final against Watford and wasn't in the squad for the big one at Wembley against Coventry, but I'd had a taste of it and, in between times, had made my full league debut against Charlton as a result of a defensive injury crisis. Gary Mabbutt was out along with Gary Stevens and Chris Hughton whilst poor old Danny Thomas's whole career was on the line as a result of a Gavin Maguire tackle a few weeks earlier against QPR; to this day, one of the worst challenges I have ever seen committed on a football field. We felt desperately sorry for Danny who was such a lovely fella but, as is often the case, one person's misfortune is somebody else's big opportunity. And it was because of injuries that my chance came along and I'd like to think I made the most of it in that game against Charlton.

Before the match, when David Pleat announced to the

press that he was going to give me my debut, he was quoted as saying: 'Neil was signed by Peter Shreeve before my arrival, but he has impressed me. He's massive with a good left foot.' Perfect credentials for a security guard then! The game itself wasn't a classic, we won 1–0 and predictably Clive Allen got the winner with his 46th goal of the season, his 31st in the league. But I thoroughly enjoyed the experience and received some glowing write-ups in the papers over the next couple of days, most notably from footballing legend Bobby Moore who said in his column: 'I was very impressed by Ruddock. He looked like Norman Hunter but with bigger muscles!' Coming from one of the best defenders the game has ever seen, I took that as a major compliment. And there were others too, with a reporter for the *Mail on Sunday* writing: 'Ruddock caught my eye with a cool perfor-mance and he looks a lad to watch.'

I missed the next game against West Ham on the Bank Holiday Monday but was back in the starting line-up two days after that for what was always going to be a grudge match against our FA Cup victims Wimbledon. They would be all out for revenge and, as we were still in third place and chasing the title, we were determined to give as good as we got. There was every chance of it 'kicking off' and, sure enough, the lads duly obliged. Mind you, Big John Gayle versus Little Nico Claesen was hardly a fair contest. Gayle was sent off for a clash with Nico, who hit the deck as if he'd been shot when Dennis Wise booted the ball in his face. Nico protested his innocence, but Dons' boss Dave Bassett criticised him in the papers for making a meal of the incident, saying: 'If that's what the continentals are going to do, they can get stuffed.' I thought it was a bit rich of Bassett to call Nico a cheat because, while some foreigners are prone to throwing themselves about a bit, he wasn't a bad lad. Some of the continentals, however, are a bit soft for my liking. Technically gifted, sure, but you wouldn't want too many of them in the trenches with you. They have never had that Millwall mentality of 'never let them know you're hurt'. Nico wasn't really a softie though, he was a feisty little so and so in fact, and we didn't call him 'Nutty Nico' for nothing.

I recall how one day big Mitchell Thomas, 'Length' as we called him for reasons I won't go into, had clattered the Belgian international who cracked us all up by chasing Mitch all the way round the training ground and threatening to flatten him. Nico also made me smile one day when we were playing in a reserve game at Tooting & Mitcham of all places. He'd only just returned from the World Cup where he had played in the semi-finals for Belgium. Suddenly he was playing what amounted to parks' football and he turned to me in disgust and said in his broken English: 'A few weeks ago I was playing in the World Cup, now I am playing at Tooting & Mitcham. What is happening to my career?'

Sadly, not a lot at White Hart Lane because, as good a player as Nico was, he just didn't fit into the 'diamond' system the team was playing at the time, with Clive Allen the sole man up front. Nico could probably have walked into most other top sides of the time and I think he became frustrated at being a bit-part player. Like he said, it wasn't that long before that he'd been playing in the World Cup finals. And it wasn't too long after that he was on his way back to Belgium. But he certainly made his mark at Spurs and made a lot of friends in the process.

The game against Wimbledon ended in a draw and

while that result wasn't too damaging in terms of the Championship, defeat at Nottingham Forest in my next first team appearance definitely was. Even though we hammered Manchester United 4–0 in our next game, our hopes of winning the league had effectively been killed off at the City Ground, and the title went to Everton, against whom I made my fourth and final appearance of that season.

The game was a meaningless one but it still caused something of a stir because David Pleat had picked what the Football League deemed to be an understrength team, even though the boss claimed we had eight people out with injuries and that it was a good opportunity to give some of the younger players in the squad a bit of experience. It was only a few days before the FA Cup final and, as Everton had already clinched the league anyway, where was the sense in risking key players? More to the point, why have a first-team squad if you can't use all the players when a manager sees fit? If a player is registered as a professional, how can it be wrong to select him? The FA Cup final was the all-important thing and, while I was a little disappointed not to be in the squad, having played a number of league games towards the end of the season, I didn't honestly expect to be involved. I was there with my Cup final suit on though, and received a silver salver for my efforts in the quarter-finals. The game against Coventry was a thriller from start to finish and, even though I was watching from the sidelines, I still got totally wrapped up in the emotion of it, thinking 'One day, I'll play in a cup final'. Clive Allen gave us the perfect start with a typical poacher's goal, his 49th of the season, but after the game had swung one way and then the other, we eventually lost out to a Gary Mabbutt own goal. You had to feel for Gary because he was such a great pro and didn't deserve that. It was a disappointing end to an exciting season but, as we'd managed to hang on to third place in the league, the signs were promising for the following year.

No sooner was the domestic season over than I was teaming up with the England Under-19 squad for a 17-day tour of South America with games against Uruguay and Brazil to look forward to. Like the trip to China the previous year, this was another fantastic opportunity to visit a country the average man in the street was only ever likely to see on *Wish You Were Here*, or whatever the holiday programme of the day was.

The samba beat, the sand, the Brazilian beauties ... they seemed to be the main topics of conversation amongst the lads as we jetted off to Rio. There were a number of players in the squad who had made the trip to China – the likes of Pressman, Thomas and Hirst – but there were plenty of new faces too; players who did go on to make it big. Paul Ince, Paul Merson and Matt Le Tissier gave the squad a lot more steel and style and you didn't have to be a rocket scientist to see that they were all destined for great things. One missing face, however, was that of my Spurs colleague David Howells who'd been to China and was desperately looking forward to having 'Rio de Janeiro' stamped on his passport. He was left out of the original party, however, and was absolutely gutted, especially as myself, Vinny Samways and John Polston kept reminding him that we were in the squad. They're a sympathetic lot, footballers. But just a few days before the squad was due to leave, David was called up as a late replacement and I have never seen anyone's face light up so dramatically.

With national team boss Bobby Robson and his number two Don Howe running the show, it was a great opportunity for me to show the main men what I was made of. Sadly, I made one hell of an impression for all the wrong reasons. What happened on that tour probably still ranks as my most embarrassing moment in football. I was sent off twice in successive matches after we were warned to be on our best behaviour by Mr Robson, no less. During the World Cup in Mexico the previous year, Ray Wilkins had been sent off against Morocco, an incident deemed to be a 'disgrace' at the time, and the England manager didn't want a repeat performance from any of his young charges on this trip.

The first dismissal, in the last minute of the game against Brazil, was an absolute joke because I was sent packing for the sort of tackle you see every five minutes in games at home. I should have known better perhaps, because the South Americans were renowned (still are, in fact) for their theatricals, and even though I'd won the ball with what I considered a firm but fair challenge, their player went down like a sack of spuds before rolling over about 14 times. It was the usual Oscar-winning performance we've come to expect from players in that part of the world. And they are supposed to be tough. The referee, who came from the same country, as was sometimes the case on junior tours of this kind, sent me off and I was absolutely devastated, even though Mr Robson was sympathetic, assuring me that these sort of occurrences were not uncommon. As for my second red card in the very next game, against Uruguay this time, that was an even bigger joke. In fact, I was the innocent party for a change because one of their players actually whacked me and, not being the sort of bloke to take things like that lying down, I squared up to him and the ref intervened before I could level the scores, so to speak. But even though I didn't get the opportunity to stick one on my opponent, the ref sent us both off.

I'd never been sent off at any level before then, in fact I don't think I'd ever been booked. I'm not saying I was an angel, because I was prone to putting myself about even in those days, but at that time bookings or yellow cards weren't dished out like they are today. You had to whack the referee or something like that to get cautioned back then.

It's difficult for players with a temper, because you get a rush of blood and do things you regret later when you've calmed down. I've always been like that although I've mellowed a little with age and experience. I've never been a thug. You don't get to play for clubs like Spurs, Liverpool and West Ham by being a nutcase.

The red cards aside, playing at places like the magnificent Maracana stadium was a great experience and we certainly had some decent players in that squad. Thankfully, I didn't really get into too much bother over the sendings off, because I think the powers-that-be recognised that I was the sort of player who always gave his all and trod a thin line. I don't think the Brazilian kids had seen anything quite like me and I think they were shocked more than hurt.

But coming a year after Wilkins had become the first English player to be sent off in the World Cup, the timing wasn't ideal and all the lads had been told in no uncertain terms to be disciplined at all times, not to get involved and, above all else, not to get sent off because the country's reputation as a footballing nation was at stake here. So what does Muggins do? Get sent off twice! But

I wasn't the only one in disgrace. After the second red card against Uruguay, I was sitting in the dressing room, head in hands, virtually in tears, thinking that was the end of my international career, when John Polston walked in and said he'd been sent off as well. Cheers, mate. Took the heat off me a little bit. We had drawn 1–1 with Brazil and beaten Uruguay 2–1, so at least the results were good even if our disciplinary record wasn't.

It was during that same summer, on a pre-season trip to Sweden with Spurs, that David Pleat came out with his immortal assessment of my ability and my future after football. He'd insisted on all the lads being in bed by a certain time on the Friday night because we had a game the following day, but his advice fell on deaf ears and all the players, including the senior and sensible pros like Hoddle and Waddle, sneaked out of the hotel at about 9 pm to find the local disco. As a 17-year-old rookie, it was my job to keep ordering the drinks and fetching them from the bar for the more seasoned drinkers. Since the well-paid members of the squad were buying me drinks to do so, I was happy to oblige. But, just as I'd ordered up 'another nine pints of lager, please' I turned around to discover that all my team-mates had suddenly vanished and just one recognisable face remained ... that of Mr Pleat. As I stood there, shame-faced and pints in hand, the manager looked me straight in the face and with a wagging finger said memorably, 'When you finish playing football, young man, which is going to be very soon I feel, you'll make a very good security guard'.

Having got on the wrong side of the manager I feared that he might give me a hard time, but fortunately Pleat was sacked soon after when compromising reports emerged about him in the press, which leads me to another story about David which still brings a wry smile to my face considering the nature of his departure and circumstances surrounding it. I can remember an incident from the same tour of Sweden, during which we had been beaten by a lower division team of part-timers, when Pleat was not a happy bunny, ranting and raving at the 'useless bunch of individuals' in front of him. Defender John Polston felt the full force of Pleat's anger as the manager launched into a tirade of abuse. 'Polston, I have got more personality in my p***k than you've got in your entire body!' Considering the stories that had been appearing in the papers, which were obviously the talk of the dressing room at the time, the players found his comments amusing to say the least and, as they desperately tried to stifle their giggles, Pleat suddenly realised the implications of his attack on Polston. The embarrassed boss left quickly after that, followed by his departure from the club not long after.

It was around this time that I first acquired the nickname of 'Razor', which has stuck with me ever since. I know it sounds intimidating, but people didn't really class me as a hard man in those early days; I was just a big, old fashioned centre-half who didn't like the idea of forwards going past me. I remember that Frank Bruno was fighting Joe Bugner at White Hart Lane during the 1987–88 season and also on the same bill was 'Razor Ruddock', a powerful Canadian boxer who took no prisoners. Most of the Spurs lads went to the fight and as a result I became known as 'Razor' thereafter. Before that I'd been known as 'Schuster', after the German player Bernd because of my prowess at free-kicks. But most of my mates and my family still call me 'Jacko' after my toy monkey (aaah!).

I got engaged to my girlfriend Sarah that summer, with the plan to wed in two years' time, and there was another big event in my life that year as Terry Venables took over as manager at White Hart Lane with the pledge of turning Tottenham into one of the biggest clubs in the country; challenging for the league title and not just the cups, for a change. Terry, who had enjoyed great success at Barcelona, was a very popular appointment with players and fans alike after David Pleat had been given the heave-ho. One paper had already revealed in the summer of 1987 that Pleat had been questioned by the police about certain illicit activities when he was in charge at Luton. That must have been embarrassing enough and although the club had stood by him on that occasion, especially after guiding us to the FA Cup final, a similar story in October later that year – which alleged that Pleat had been caught out again by the vice squad – left Spurs with little alternative but to terminate his contract.

There was a lot of speculation about who might take his place but, as Terry had already ended his reign in Spain, he was the red-hot favourite and the man we all wanted in the hot-seat. His track record as a top coach spoke for itself and the players were convinced he could take us on to greater things. From a personal point of view, I was delighted with the appointment because at that time Terry had a reputation for giving young, inexperienced players a chance and obviously I came into that category, so I hoped my Tottenham career would really take off under him. The initial signs were certainly encouraging as he put me in the starting line-up for his first proper game in charge, at home to Liverpool in front of a massive 47,000 crowd at White Hart Lane.

Terry had agreed to join us some time before then, but he insisted on taking a planned holiday in America before taking up the reins. Because we were in the middle of a bad run of seven games without a win, however, he cut short his vacation to try and arrest the slide and the match with Liverpool was quite an occasion. It certainly was for me. I'd played in a couple of games just prior to that and caretaker boss Doug Livermore had gone on record as saying that I'd done really well in the two matches I'd started: both draws against Portsmouth and QPR. So I was delighted to be named in Terry's first side and was full of optimism, especially as he'd been so supportive and encouraging during a one-to-one chat I'd had with him after he'd taken over full time. He told me that I'd be given every chance to prove myself, like the rest of the lads, and he made me believe I had the ability to be a real success at White Hart Lane. I just couldn't wait to start playing for the man.

Terry's first game against Liverpool was a bit of a disaster, however, because we had Steve Hodge sent off after just 17 minutes for elbowing Ray Houghton in the face. Steve wasn't exactly renowned as a tough guy, so his actions were surprising to say the least. Sheer frustration on his part, I guess. Terry wasn't too impressed, either, with Steve's challenge or the red card decision. He thought a yellow card would have sufficed. But we all know what can happen when you raise your arm at an opponent in the way Steve did. One paper described 'Hodgy' as 'stupid, peevish and unprofessional' which was a little bit over the top, but it was unnecessary and put us under a lot of pressure against a decent Liverpool side with 70-odd minutes remaining. We managed to hold out for an hour, but they broke us down twice in the last 30 minutes as we tired and we ended up losing 2–0. Not the best start for Terry, and a disastrous afternoon for me because I'd picked up an injury which X-rays later revealed was a broken ankle. It was a result of what is traditionally known as a 'crunching' tackle by Liverpool's Gary Gillespie and, although I was in a fair amount of pain as I hobbled off for treatment, I didn't think it was too serious. I managed to complete the game – all part of the tough-guy image I was developing – and even when I had an X-ray straight afterwards it didn't reveal anything. It wasn't until a week or so later, when it was still troubling me, that a second X-ray showed that the bone in my ankle was badly fractured and that I would need an operation.

I couldn't believe my bad luck because, with a new man in charge, I was desperate to make a good impression, yet suddenly I was going to be sidelined for a couple of months after playing just one game for Terry. The boss had been full of praise for my performance in that game and I certainly felt comfortable out there, even in such distinguished company. Terry described Gillespie's challenge as 'a bad tackle' but I'm not so sure and I wasn't about to start whingeing about it in the papers, or anything like that. Live by the sword, die by the sword, as they say.

It was the first serious injury I'd ever had and it couldn't have come at a worse time and, although the boss offered loads of words of sympathy and encouragement, I was very down for a while. Thankfully, there were no complications with the operation and I was soon back in training and knocking on the first team door once more. I only made a couple more appearances for Spurs that season – one in the FA Cup against Port Vale when I scored in an embarrassing Fourth Round defeat – and the summer brought more disappointment with the news that Terry was selling me back to my old club Millwall for £300,000, quite a profit as far as Spurs were concerned. Lots of changes were going on at the time, with Ossie Ardiles going on loan to Blackburn and the new boss strengthening his first-team squad with a number of signings, the biggest being the £2 million capture of a certain Paul Gascoigne. But as Gazza was coming in one door, I was going out of another; my Spurs career over – for the time being, at least.

CHAPTER FIVE

How the Dell Boy Became a Man

The summer of 1988 was a strange one really because having had a couple of years to settle in at Spurs, made a bit of an impression and seemingly struck a chord with the manager I still consider to be the best in the business, I was looking forward to a relaxing break before preparing for what was going to be the most important season of my career to date. Not that Terry Venables' decision to accept an offer from my old club Millwall came as a complete surprise. There had been lots of speculation in the press and around the club for some time that Terry was going to make changes at the end of the 1987–88 season, stamp his authority on the club and bring in his kind of players. He'd already signed an old favourite in Terry Fenwick, who has been virtually everywhere with him over the years, and there was talk that a deal to bring Paul McGrath to White Hart Lane was as good as signed and sealed.

The boss wanted experience at the heart of his defence and, at this stage of my career, I didn't exactly fit the bill. It wasn't that he didn't rate me as 'one for the future' as they say, in fact I knew he thought a lot of me, it was just that he wanted quality performers with know-how, immediately. There was an offer of a new, improved contract on the table for me at the time so that was good enough reason to believe he felt I had a future at Tottenham, but he did warn me that I could spend the next season or two in the reserves, banging on the door of the first team again and hoping for another break. I'd already been through that and wasn't sure I could spend another couple of years waiting for the sort of chance Terry had given me that season when the broken ankle in my first game against Liverpool stopped me in my ambitious tracks. I wanted first team football and, even though I was only 20 at the time and loved Spurs, and Terry Venables in particular, I wasn't prepared to wait around. I spoke to the manager on a number of occasions and he didn't want me to go, but he did say that if I moved on I wouldn't be considered a Tottenham failure. So I took heed of Tel's advice that 'sometimes you have to take a step down to come back up'.

Not that returning to Millwall was a backward step at all. My old club had just won promotion to Division One for the first time in their history and the place was buzzing; even happier than I remembered it as a kid. Suddenly, Millwall FC were being taken seriously for a change – and for all the right reasons this time.

Before the opportunity to go back to my first club had materialised, Terry had arranged for me to have talks with Portsmouth where his old friend Jim Gregory was the chairman, so off I went down to the South Coast and although it would have meant dropping down a division, I was quite impressed with what he had to say. I told Jim I'd get back to him with my decision and, in the meantime, Millwall must have got wind of the fact that Spurs were looking to offload me because Bob Pearson, the chief scout who had known me as a kid, phoned me and asked how I felt about 'coming home' and that was that, really.

I didn't want to leave Spurs because it was a massive club full of superstars, but I got a few bob for signing on for Millwall, with a decent four-year contract, and I was still in the top flight with a better chance of first team football. At least, that's what I thought at the time. Even though Millwall had forked out what was then a club record £300,000 fee, manager John Docherty did explain to me pretty early on that he would be sticking initially with the team which had won promotion from the Second Division and I could fully understand his thinking behind that. The players who had worked so hard to get the club into the top flight – people like Tony Cascarino, Teddy Sheringham, Alan McLeary and good old Terry Hurlock – deserved their chance to prove themselves against the best in the country, and they certainly did that. It was a strange situation to be in, because you want the team to do well and make a good impression when everyone else in the country thought we'd be relegation certainties, but I also realised that for me to get a chance in the first XI we needed to be on the end of a couple of bad results. As it turned out, the lads stormed to the top of the table against all odds and expectations on the back of an eight-match unbeaten run. It was an incredible time for the club, the best in its history even now, and as a supporter as well as a player I was delighted to see the team which had been my life since I was a boy sitting there on top of the pile looking down on the likes of Liverpool and Manchester United. But even though I'd been named as sub a couple of times, without getting on, I didn't feel part of that early success and the adulation which went with it. Already I was beginning to wonder if I had made the right decision in leaving Spurs. I couldn't really complain though, because I'd been brought back as a centre-half and the two lads at the back at the time, Alan McLeary and Steve Wood, were playing out of their skins. So was everyone else, especially the two front men, Teddy and Tony Cas, who scored eight goals in the first seven league games. Me, I didn't even get a kick until the 78th minute of the ninth game against Nottingham Forest –and then it was as an emergency striker, a position I hadn't played in since my first spell at The Den. But desperate situations call for desperate measures and, as we were 2–0 down at the time, throwing another big lump on up front seemed to be the only option left. We didn't expect Forest to come at us the way they had; we probably thought they would be something of a soft touch at The Den, but they put us under a lot of pressure and with 12 minutes to go it was my chance to come on and break them down. Although I considered myself a defender I was just happy to be involved, and I was positively ecstatic less than ten minutes later when I rose at the far post to score the equaliser after Teddy had pulled one back within a minute of me making my entrance. Inspired substitution, or what?

It was an amazing feeling, but as it had been so long since I'd actually scored a goal in front of a big crowd, I wasn't quite sure how to celebrate. So, in time-honoured

Millwall fashion, I just went mental, as did everyone inside The Den that day –including Forest boss Brian Clough, who was doing his nut on the line after seeing his side throw away a 2–0 lead. I savoured every inch of that 60-yard celebratory jig and in that one moment all the disappointment of being left out of the side, and the frustration at being played out of position at centre-forward in the reserves disappeared, briefly at least.

I remember Steve Hodge, who got both Forest goals, saying afterwards that in those closing stages it was like 'defending the Alamo' and we certainly bombarded them with everything we'd got. It was a typical Millwall performance in the last ten minutes or so and we got our rewards for showing the never-say-die spirit which had taken us to the top and become our trademark. The draw with Forest was our eighth game in the league without defeat and we had the proud distinction of being the only unbeaten team in the country; an incredible run which came to an end a week later when we lost away at Middlesbrough. Once again I was on the bench; once again I was brought on as a striker to try and save the game and by now I was getting thoroughly pissed off with the whole situation, especially as John Docherty had gone on record as saying, 'Ruddock is the best finisher at the club', suggesting that was my best position. I knew it wasn't and I knew my future was as a stopper, not a scorer. Not that I helped my personal situation by bagging two more goals in a striking role against Gillingham and another cracker against Aston Villa in the Littlewoods Cup around the same time.

Goal-scoring did come naturally to me and, because the management – reserve team coach Roger Cross aside – remembered me as a big, powerful front man from my first spell, that's where they seemed hell-bent on playing me. Being a stroppy so-and-so, even at that young age, I was equally determined I was going to play at the back and that was why I slammed in a transfer request just a few months after I had become the club's record signing. The worst moment came a few weeks after I'd made my only first team appearances of the season. I was left out of the squad totally for the away game at Derby and told to report for duty with the reserves, which I did only to find out that I wasn't wanted by them either. From that moment on, Docherty and I never saw eye-to-eye, although reports of us having a series of bust-ups were exaggerated in the local press. Just. I stated my case, he stood his ground and that was the beginning of the end for me and Millwall. People tried to come up with all sorts of reasons why Docherty wanted to get rid of me, but the truth of the matter was that he saw me as a target man and I saw myself as a defender who could play a bit. End of story. I was very disillusioned with the whole situation and even though I was scoring goals in the reserves, I still wasn't happy. I'd scored something like eight in 11 games, but while that record was impressive, it wasn't doing me any favours in terms of getting a first team place in the position I wanted to play.

Ironically, the turning point for me came when we played Southampton's second team in February 1989 and I was playing at the back for a change, charged with the task of marking a cocky, young upstart called Alan Shearer whom we'd heard was a bit tasty. Roger Cross, the reserve team boss, knew I wanted to play at the back and he was one of the few people to show faith in me in that position. Although Docherty thought otherwise, Roger always told me to stick to my guns, be stubborn and concentrate on being a defender and it was thanks to him that I got my move to Southampton on the strength of my performance against this wonderkid Shearer, who was only a baby at the time. I battered Alan, who later became my best mate in football, all over the place and gave him a really hard time that day. I even found an opportunity to steal forward and score in what was a comfortable win, while he hardly had a kick. I still wind Shearer up about that game to this day and keep telling him that because he was so crap, I stood out and Southampton were so impressed that they signed me the next day. If he'd been any good, I probably wouldn't have got the move. Thanks Al, you made me!

Everything happened so quickly after that because Southampton were on the phone the next morning inquiring about me and it was better for both parties that I moved on to a club that wanted me to play in my favourite role. Millwall got their money back so everyone was happy. Docherty had always said that he wouldn't keep players who were unsettled, so it angered me to learn that he'd previously turned down a £300,000 bid from Southampton and that made me lose my rag with him even more. 'If you don't want me, sell me,' I'd plead with him and it was at that time I lost respect for the man because he had turned me against the club I loved. I only found out through the former Millwall player Bryan King, a great goalkeeper in his day, who was now an agent and he knew that Southampton had been in for me before. 'Kingy' didn't want to act as my agent, he just wanted me to know that things were going on behind my back. I was disappointed in the club because Docherty had promised to keep me informed and had gone back on his word. He said it was because Millwall wanted to keep me and that he didn't want me alerted to the fact that another First Division club was expressing an interest. But I'd already made my mind up by then that I was going to move on and, sure enough, it was next stop Southampton. I can be a stubborn so-and-so at times and once I've made a decision in my own mind, nothing or no-one is going to budge me from it. My heart was set on moving because I felt betrayed.

And even though the club (Millwall) had started the season so well, I wasn't the only discontented member of the squad. A number of the senior players had begun to realise that they were getting paid peanuts compared to most of their opponents in the top division and there was a lot of resentment that they weren't receiving the rewards for their efforts. Teddy Sheringham, in particular, knew he could have his pick of the big clubs and there was talk about Glasgow Rangers and Aberdeen watching him with a view to making a bid. I guess that's why he refused to sign the new contract which the club had begrudgingly offered him. Teddy was the best player at Millwall, a class act and someone I respected and admired, and he knew his true worth even if the club didn't.

It wasn't that he was cocky or arrogant, he was just confident in his own ability. Even though he was only a little older than me, Teddy was my hero and I still rate him as one of the most intelligent players I've come across in the English game. He was a nice bloke too and, like John Fashanu before him, he was great with the younger, less experienced players at the club; always prepared to offer advice and encouragement – and give those without cars a lift to and from training from time to time. He was a smooth character, a bit flash some might say, but the lads at Millwall never had a bad word to say about him. He was somebody to look up to and I'm delighted that, after a long and distinguished career, he's finally getting the rewards his talents deserve.

It was suggested that my decision to ask for a transfer would spark off a full-scale player revolt but my gripe wasn't about money, it was about my role as a professional within the club. Either way, Docherty eventually agreed to let me go to a club that desperately wanted a centre-half to plug a defence which was leaking goals all over the shop after starting the season so well themselves. The Saints had just conceded ten goals in their previous two games and were in the middle of what was to prove to be the worst run in the club's history. Which was where I came in.

It proved to be a fantastic move for me and, while I was a little sad to leave all my mates at The Den, I had to get away for the sake of my career. It soon struck me what a friendly, family club Southampton was and I enjoyed working for the manager, Chris Nicholl, who was an exceptional centre-half in his day and taught me a lot. He used to give me a bit of stick, and rightly so, for getting into trouble with referees for querying decisions and generally being a bit lippy ('I've got a letter from the FA; you've got to shut it!').

Chris was under a lot of pressure at the time I joined the club because, even though he'd won a Manager of the Month award earlier in the season, his team later went 20-odd games without a win and were plummeting towards the bottom of the table at an alarming rate. There was talk at the time of Lawrie McMenemy returning to the club where he had enjoyed so much success earlier in his managerial career and that annoyed Chris who couldn't see the point in the club and the media bringing even more pressure to bear. It was bad enough as it was. Thankfully, we managed to arrest the slide before it was too late and I'd like to think I played quite an important role in the revival which was to keep the club in the top flight at a time when relegation was seriously on the cards. I'd made my Southampton debut on 18 February 1989 in a 1–1 draw at Sheffield Wednesday and slowly but surely we began to shore things up at the back with yours truly settling in nicely alongside Russell Osman after Kevin Moore had been dropped and made something of a scapegoat by fans who had become more than a little anxious about the threat to the club's First Division status.

Kevin was a great pro and even though this young kid had come to the club and claimed his first team place he was brilliant to me, passing on advice and generally helping me settle into the team. I can't speak highly enough of him. In hindsight, I don't think I could have gone to a better club to learn my trade, because there were so many good professionals around me.

Although the team wasn't conceding as many goals as it had around the turn of the year, we were still losing games until it came to a crunch, bottom of the table clash with Newcastle when I became an overnight hero with the Saints' fans in the most unlikely of circumstances – as a penalty king in the last minute of a real, relegation nail-biter. It had been a bit of a gamble going to a club which was on a real downer, but when I arrived and had a look around the dressing room I knew there was too much talent and experience for Southampton to get relegated.

People like Osman, Jimmy Case, Glenn Cockerill,

Barry Horne and Micky Adams were not going to let the club go down without a fight. We just needed a bit of a break and we got it against Newcastle when we were awarded what was considered a dubious penalty in the dying seconds after Kenny Sansom was deemed to have brought down Rodney Wallace. As soon as the penalty was awarded, I looked around and could see that not too many of our lads fancied it. So I decided to take it upon myself to grab the ball and assume responsibility for the kick myself, even though I wasn't a penalty taker, and Matt Le Tissier wasn't in the side that day. Thankfully, my confidence wasn't misplaced and I smashed the ball home to give us a precious victory which enabled us to end the club's dismal run without a win, turn the corner, and, ultimately, avoid the drop. Suddenly, I was the big hero, although after the game my Dad came up to me in the players' lounge and said, 'Don't ever put me through that again'. It was a nerve-racking moment for everyone except me, it seemed. In the next game I scored two more in a 3–3 draw at Middlesbrough and from then on my goal celebration became known as the 'Ruddock Stomp' and the fans really took to me. They even had T-shirts and posters made in my honour.

Our confidence grew after that and when we beat Aston Villa and Manchester United in successive games, we were safe with a game to go and the celebration party began, with me being virtually stripped naked as I left the field at the end of the United match. I can remember seeing grown men and women crying in the stands and I'd like to think they have never forgotten me down there for the contribution I made so early in my Southampton career. It was the start of a long and happy relationship with some of the nicest people I have met in football. Big

Les, who ran the bar in the players' lounge, still keeps my two-pint glass on the top shelf for when I'm playing at The Dell. I got married to Sarah that summer so things couldn't have been better.

There were some great characters at the club too; notably John 'Budgie' Burridge, the keeper, who was quite simply different class. I'd heard a few stories about him being a bit of a nutter, and I wasn't disappointed. The first thing I noticed about playing just in front of him was that he used to do a running commentary of the game from the edge of his penalty box. You'd receive the ball from him, turn away from goal and suddenly hear this voice behind you. 'Burridge, rolls it out to Ruddock, who slips the ball through to Le Tissier, who...' And that's how he would go on throughout the match; it was his way of maintaining his concentration. Even when he was involved in the action himself, he would shout out things like 'and that's another magnificent save by Burridge'. Another favourite line of his, designed to cause panic in the calmest of back fours, was when a ball was played over the top of our defence and you would hear him yell at the top of his voice 'KEEPERS...!' before adding a second or so later '...NOT COMING!' He obviously wasn't all there because, as I experienced at first hand, he was just as crazy at home where he would get his wife to throw oranges for him to catch as he sat in the lounge with his goalkeeping gloves on. He would encourage her to throw them when he was least expecting it to test his reflexes. Mad! Better still, he used to go to bed on a Friday night wearing his gloves and clutching a ball as a pre-match ritual.

He was a great character to have around the place and for a 40-year-old he was as fit as a flea. He was always working out, always going through some routine or other. Mind you, there was one occasion when his eccentric approach to training almost caused him some serious damage. One day he came into the training ground carrying a three-foot long steel rod and a set of six-inch nails, and proceeded to pin the bar to the wall so he could do some pull-ups in his spare time. Not exactly the actions of a normal human being, but this is 'Budgie' we're talking about. Everything seemed to be going according to plan and, with the bar in place, he decided to test the makeshift apparatus by leaping into the air and grabbing the metal pole with both hands. As soon as he did so, there was mad panic in the room as John began shaking violently and screaming at the top of his voice. We thought he was just messing around as usual, but it turned out that he'd hammered one of the nails through an electric cable in the wall and given himself a massive shock once he grabbed hold of the steel bar. He was quite badly shaken but, ultimately, none the worse for his experience; and definitely none the wiser.

Sadly, 'Budgie' moved on the following season but was replaced by another terrific fella and great goalkeeper in Tim Flowers who certainly played his part in the most successful campaign the club had enjoyed since the Lawrie Mac–Kevin Keegan era.

Tim was a smashing lad, although nowhere near as crazy as his predecessor. But just as one nutter was leaving, another was arriving in the shape of a player who became a great friend of mine, Barry Horne. A totally different character to 'Budgie' but game for a laugh nevertheless; as I discovered during a mid-season break in Portugal. It happened to be his birthday while we were away so, having celebrated in the usual way, I helped Barry back to his room as he was a little worse for wear. When we got there 'Elvis', as he became known for his love of 'The King', decided it would be a good idea to launch himself into a diving header, using the very nice, fabric lampshade hanging in the middle of the room as a ball.

It was a magnificent dive alright and would have been a great 'goal' but for one slight problem; the 'nice, fabric lampshade' wasn't made totally of fabric. The inside was made of solid steel hanging from a metal chain and Elvis ended up having four stitches inserted in a nasty head wound.

On the field, we had played some great stuff that 1989–90 season, and were never out of the top half of the table, finishing a creditable seventh despite losing the last two games of the league campaign against Arsenal and Spurs. A couple of wins in those games and we could have reached as high as third but, either way, it was a fantastic achievement by a team which was inspired by the brilliance of Matt Le Tissier who really came into his own that season, scoring 20 goals – most of them typical Le Tiss efforts. Must have been something to do with his pre-match meal, which used to consist of a Double Whopper with large fries from Burger King, all washed down with a couple of pints of coke. In fact, I can remember on the day of our biggest game of the season – at home to Liverpool who were flying high in those days – there was me, Le Tiss, Barry Horne and Mickey Adams all filling our faces at the local McDonald's just a couple of hours before kick-off. Most players' pre-match meal consisted of chicken, fish or pasta but ours was a burger and fries! We were all in hysterics when Barry piped up with 'Do you think John

Barnes, Ian Rush and the boys will be tucking into a McDonald's?'

Highly unlikely, but the unusual preparations obviously didn't do us any harm because we turned in our best performance of the season to beat the mighty Reds 4–1 to go third in the table. Jason Dodd, who had just joined the club from non-league and was playing in only his second game, was outstanding that day and virtually marked the great Barnesy out of the match, and he will never forget how John came into the dressing room after what was a crushing defeat by Liverpool standards to shake his hand and congratulate him.

Le Tissier, without doubt the most technically gifted pro I have ever played with, was *the* man that season, even though Alan Shearer was starting to make his mark in the side. We all knew 'Shocksy' was destined for something special even though he was never a prolific scorer in the first team at Southampton. In fact, I beat him in the scoring stakes that season with four goals to his three, as I went to great lengths to remind him on occasions afterwards. He quickly became my best mate at the club and it's a little ironic to think that, in the early days, I would drive him everywhere because he didn't have a car and even lent him money from time to time because he was always skint. Now look at him! He was my first regular room-mate and, although people have this impression of him these days as being a bit dour and straight (okay, boring!), I know he's got a wicked sense of humour and we always had a great laugh – apart from the time we almost wrecked his career on what proved to be a rather boisterous summer tour of Portugal. It still makes me cringe to think about it, and what might have been, even now.

We nicknamed him 'Shocksy', because when he first started out, that's what he used to do: shock people by scoring or doing something special every time he stepped up a level, either for Southampton or England. Like the time he scored a hat-trick against Arsenal on his full first-team debut for the Saints. But the biggest shock of all, for Alan and those of us involved, came during a boozy, holiday prank which went horribly wrong. It wasn't particularly unusual for end-of-season trips to turn into all-day binges and this one, at a time when Alan was still in his teens, was no exception. On this occasion, however, the repercussions were far from funny and ended with our young star being rushed to a Portuguese hospital. Let me explain.

The order of the day was to get up reasonably early, play golf, go to the beach, have a few drinks, etc. One night we'd gone back to our rooms and me, Mickey Adams, Barry Horne and Matt Le Tissier had all drunk our mini-bars dry, so we thought, 'Whose can we raid?' Shocksy's, of course. He wasn't a big drinker at the time so we knew there'd be plenty of booze left in his fridge. Off we went to his room. He was half asleep in the bath at the time, so while Barry was busy yanking the mini-bar off the wall and marching down the corridor –with all the glasses still on top – I was pouring a bottle of vodka all over Alan in the bath. Needless to say he wasn't very amused, especially as the vodka had gone in his eyes and was causing him some discomfort. So he leapt out of the bath and began chasing us down the corridor … with nothing on. As Barry tried to get away, with mini-bar in tow, all the glasses were falling off and breaking on the floor behind him as he went. Alan, in his rage, didn't notice the broken glass and as I looked round I could see him heading straight for it, but before I could say 'Mind the glass' he'd trampled all the way through it and collapsed to the floor in agony with blood pouring from his feet.

The sight of him lying there in a right mess sobered us up instantly and there was mass panic as we tried to work out what to do. I really started to worry when I looked down at his feet and saw three of his toes, cut to the bone and hanging on by a thread. We knew we had to get him off to hospital quick to save his toes, but the trouble was no-one was sober enough to drive. Even the coaching staff were incapable of driving. The only person in any fit state was Steve Davis, who rushed Shocksy off to hospital. When we got there, the hospital was like something out of the 1920s, and nothing like the those at home. Alan was just left in a room with no curtains or anything like that, with car accident victims in one corner, people with broken legs in another, and poor old Alan wondering what the hell was going on and how they were going to save his toes. It was a close run thing, but they managed to stitch him back up and after a while he was as good as new.

Heaven knows how close he came to losing his toes altogether and, if that had been the case, his career could have ended all too prematurely. And all because he was the innocent victim of a drunken prank. And *he* hadn't even been drinking. Poor old boy, there he was having a quiet soak in the bath and the next minute he's got all these lunatics raiding his room and soaking him in vodka. You can look back and laugh about it now, but at the time we were bricking ourselves because anything could have happened.

Thankfully, Alan emerged relatively unscathed and

we've all seen what he's gone on to achieve. Even as a kid you could see he had the makings of a top-quality striker and while he didn't score that many goals for Saints, his work-rate and passion for the game was unbelievable. And he would be the first to tell you that he did Le Tissier's running for about three or four seasons before he got his inevitable big-money move to Blackburn. He's since learned the art of letting other lesser mortals do his running for him, while he's made something of a habit of sticking the ball in the back of the net. Off the field, he's a great bloke too. He wouldn't have become my best mate otherwise. People have got this view of him as being dull and boring, but when you get to know him, his true character comes out and he's good fun to be around; not at all like his public image. He may come across as reserved and ultra-conservative when he's being interviewed, but that's probably more down to his mistrust of the media and the way some reporters can misconstrue things than his own personality. He plays his cards close to his chest, doesn't give anything away and I think the way he handles the publicity, being such a high-profile figure who is open to criticism, is brilliant. Get him away from the football field, away from the microphones and cameras, and you see a different man entirely. We keep in regular touch and, while we've had the odd run-in as opponents since we both left Southampton, we still get on famously today. As do our respective families.

As for me, it was during the 1989–90 season that I first began running into trouble with referees; not so much because of bad tackles or being overly-aggressive but mainly for dissent or back-chatting – petty offences which Chris Nicholl used to hate. I can remember him being quoted in the papers as saying that so many of my bookings were 'futile' and 'pointless' and, to a large extent, he was right. I got suspended a couple of times, for running up 21 and 30 points, and missed about ten games in total. I vowed to try and keep my temper under control and avoid silly cautions, but I certainly didn't want to lose the power and the passion which were such important aspects of my game. If I'd lost them, there wouldn't have been much left and I might as well have followed David Pleat's advice and become a security guard. It was a case of channelling my aggression and I succeeded in doing that the following season, 1990–91, when I was virtually an ever-present in a struggling side which just managed to avoid relegation. I only served one two-match suspension as a result of picking up a needless booking for stealing a few yards at a free-kick. Hardly a hanging offence but pretty stupid nonetheless, as manager Nicholl pointed out once again. I felt I was learning though.

The following year, my last at Southampton, was when things started to go horribly wrong, however, and that was a shame because, having captained the England Under-20s in 1990, I'd made a decent impression in the Under-21s and my career was progressing along the right lines. I was already being talked about as a future England centre-half at that stage, but little more than a few months later I'd earned myself a reputation of an entirely different kind. Suddenly my club career, let alone my international future, was on the line…

CHAPTER SIX

From Saint to Sinner

After three and a half brilliant years down on the South Coast with Southampton, I almost blew everything I'd worked for in the space of a mad, six-month spell which saw me branded virtually everything from a thug to a headcase; a reputation I honestly felt would never go away and would ultimately destroy my career. Sounds dramatic, I know, but when you've been sent off twice before Christmas – once for head-butting an opponent – booked nine times, banned three times and transfer-listed by a manager who'd run out of patience, you do begin to wonder whether the whole world is against you. Especially as the papers had made me out to be the biggest villain since Jack the Ripper.

The season hadn't started too well as I was sent off for a professional foul on my old Southampton team-mate Rodney Wallace who had just moved to Leeds. Rod was clean through and I had little or no option but to bring him down and, with the new ruling, I had to walk. That offence alone wasn't too damning but, after coming back, picking up a few yellow cards and being suspended for a couple of games during November, I completely lost the plot in a game against Notts County just before Christmas. It was 20 December 1991 to be precise; the day I thought my whole world had caved in.

It was a bit ironic really because in the days leading up to the game I'd had a few chats with manager Ian Branfoot about the prospect of a new contract as my present deal was due to run out at the end of the season. It was coming up to Christmas and he promised that we would open up talks early in the New Year, which was reassuring because I was really happy at the club and was ready to commit for a few more years, providing the deal was right, obviously. Money wasn't the biggest motivating factor, it never has been during my career despite what some people might suggest, but my next contract was a very important one for me and I wanted to make sure everything was spot on. I had never hinted that I wanted to move anywhere else and it seemed the club was happy to extend my stay on the South Coast. The family was happy and settled, which was important too. So everything seemed set fair and, with Christmas coming up plus the prospect of a new deal, things couldn't have been much better.

But one rush of blood against Notts County put an end to all that and left me feeling lower than Craig Short after I'd sent him crashing to the ground with a head-butt as all hell broke loose at The Dell. There was only a minute left in the game and no need for me to get involved in an incident which didn't concern me, but they had just equalised and I was getting wound-up when Short was involved in a bit of a ruck with Alan Shearer inside the County half. I was convinced I saw their player stamp on Shocksy when he went down, and that was it – the red mist came down and I stormed about 50 yards down the field on a revenge mission. It all ended with me head-butting Short, who needed four stitches in a nasty wound above his eye, and it was no real surprise when I was shown the red card.

I didn't need telling that I'd been stupid and gone completely over the top this time, but nothing much was said after the game about an incident which was to completely change the course of my career. It was not until the following lunchtime when it dawned on me how much trouble I was in. Branfoot called the restaurant where I was eating at the time to tell me that I was going to be fined and transfer-listed by the club. What the FA was going to do about it was anybody's guess at that point. All I could think about after my conversation with the manager was that I had wrecked everything that I had worked for and I felt sick to the pit of my stomach. It certainly put me off my lunch, I can tell you. In fact, it ruined my whole Christmas because the papers were full of stories basically saying that there was no place in football for a thug like me. Branfoot had left me in no doubt that, as far as Southampton Football Club was concerned, my behaviour had been 'totally unacceptable' and that my only course of action was to find another club – if anyone would have me. I knew what I had done was wrong, but I thought I might have got some sort of support from my manager and from the club which I had served pretty well. I asked Branfoot at the time if it was his decision to boot me out and he maintained that it was, although I'm sure that he was getting leaned on from above to take the proper action to ensure that Southampton's reputation as a squeaky-clean, family club remained intact. It was as if they were saying, 'We don't do things like this at The Dell' and, as popular as I was with the fans at the time, I had to pay the ultimate price. It was a worrying time for me and, of course, I regretted what I did, but we all make mistakes. I know I've never been an angel, but that was my first major indiscretion for violent conduct and I thought I could have been given a second chance. The irony of it all is that I ended up getting a dream move back to Spurs, followed by another dream move to Liverpool soon after. If it had never happened, I would probably have ended up signing a new contract with Southampton and fighting relegation battles, and a few more opponents no doubt, for the rest of my career. It's strange how things work out.

At the time I couldn't see all that light at the end of the tunnel, though. Branfoot went to great lengths to tell me that I'd been stupid and had screwed up my career, and he couldn't see another club taking me on. Thanks, boss. He made it a personal thing and rammed the message home that I wasn't wanted by ordering me to train with the kids so, as you can imagine, I was at an all-time low. By making such a big deal of it, and publicly announcing that I had been put on the transfer list, Southampton made the matter twice as bad as it was and gave the media every excuse to make an example of me. But my family and friends stuck by me, even if my manager didn't, and they helped me get through a difficult time in my career. My old team-mate Jimmy Case was the one who did more than anyone to keep me from going under. There were times when I felt like walking away from it all but, even though he had left the club, Jimmy still took the time to phone me on occasions to lift my spirits and encourage me to keep going. He told me I was a good enough player, and a strong enough character, to dig my way out of this and he told me not to take too much notice of what was being written about me. I certainly remembered his words of wisdom.

Having been fined and transfer-listed by the club, I was hauled up before the FA to explain my actions and must have made a pretty good job of my defence because I escaped a 'disrepute' charge, which was a relief, although I obviously had to serve the customary ban for the sending off. And, after a long period of anxiety, worry, depression and uncertainty, I was also given a reprieve by Branfoot who recalled me to the side after I'd served my time in the stiffs. He seemed to be impressed with the way I'd knuckled down in training, even though I wasn't involved with the first team. I'd made a conscious effort to keep my nose clean and work hard, and I think he recognised that I was doing my best to get my career back on track. I don't think recalling me to the side was a case of Branfoot backing down after taking such strong action against me because, as I said earlier, I don't think the decision to drop me and transfer list me was entirely his. I had responded the right way, in a positive and professional manner, and for that I owe a great debt of gratitude to Ray Graydon, now a successful manager in his own right, who was in charge of the kids I had been forced to train with at the time. He did a magnificent job in keeping my spirits up when I was feeling desperately low, and he was always full of encouragement and reassurance. 'Keep your head up, work hard and they will come round, son,' he used to tell me; and they did. Thanks to Ray, by the time I was recalled to the first team I was super-fit, physically, and mentally stronger too. I will never forget what he did for me, and I'm delighted he's achieved so much at Walsall because he is one of the game's genuine nice guys.

The team went on a great run after my return – winning six games on the spin at one point – and I certainly played my part to the extent that, suddenly, the manager was my best mate again and now wanted me to sign a new contract which would virtually have doubled my salary. But that was never really an option after what had happened; there'd been too much water under the bridge. And, in any case, because I was performing so well, so consistently, and without getting into any more trouble, a number of clubs were coming down to The Dell to watch me as they knew my contract was up at the end of the season and I was ignoring the temptation of signing a new deal. Spurs were one of the teams showing an interest in me and that was a massive shot in the arm after thinking previously that no-one would touch me with a barge pole following the Craig Short incident and all the negative publicity that followed it. Thankfully, people had forgotten about that and were more concerned about what I could do with my feet rather than my head. Yet even though I knew my Southampton career was coming to an end and that I would be moving on, wherever, at the end of the season I continued to give my all for the club, for the fans in particular. They had been brilliant to me throughout the time I was out of the side and I wanted to pay them back for the incredible support and faith they had shown in me. It was never going to be a case of me simply 'seeing out' my existing contract. I was going to give my all.

Once I was back in the team and the manager was behind me once more, I found myself forgiving Branfoot – although not enough to sign a new contract. I was angry with him at the time, hurt as well, but in the main he was a good manager and had the respect of the players whom he encouraged to socialise together in order to maintain the great team spirit we always had at Southampton. He loved the lads going out as a group, having a few beers and generally enjoying ourselves when the work was done. In fact, he used to organise trips abroad on a regular basis – every few months – and I can remember him saying 'You'll be drinking in bars all over the world if you do well for me and the club'. In that respect, he was a good manager and I have to admire him for the fact that, ultimately, he did let bygones be bygones and give me my place back in the side. People seem to forget that, for the most part, we were scrapping away against relegation for much of my time at The Dell and that every tackle, not just every game, was important. It was a case of roll up your sleeves and die for the cause; that's the way it was.

Doing my best for the team and proving a lot of people wrong was the all-important thing at that time, particularly as we were in the middle of a great FA Cup run and on course for a Wembley appearance, albeit in the Zenith Data Systems Cup. It was only a two-bob competition, but the further you go and the closer you get to the Twin Towers, the more you start taking it seriously. But it was in the FA Cup that we had really begun to feel that Wembley was beckoning, especially after an amazing penalty shoot-out victory over Manchester United at Old Trafford in a fourth round replay which still stands out in the memory. We had gone 2–0 up, and looked pretty good in the process, but you can never count United out – especially at home – and with a huge crowd behind them, they pulled the scores level with about a minute to go. After a goalless period of extra-time came the dreaded penalty shoot-out; not that I was too worried. I stepped up to take the first spot-kick, right in front of a baying Stretford End, and as calm as you like sent Peter Schmeichel the wrong way. Then Neil Webb fluffed their first kick and, as he was a former Portsmouth player, you can imagine the delight of our small but noisy travelling army of fans. Ryan Giggs missed another for United and we were through without our last kicker, Matt Le Tissier, having to step forward. Needless to say, the celebrations were something special and it was after beating one of the favourites that we began to think our name just might be on the cup. But, after making hard work of getting past Third Division Bolton in the next round, we were knocked out by Norwich in the quarter-finals, after another replay. Getting to Wembley for the FA Cup Final would have been the ideal way to finish my spell with Southampton but it wasn't meant to be, although we did have a good day out at the ZDS Cup Final which we lost 3–2 to Nottingham Forest – Teddy Sheringham and all – after coming back from two goals down. Even if we had made it to the FA Cup Final, I doubt I would have been fit enough to play as I had damaged my calf muscle with a few games to go and that was the end of my season and my spell as a Saint.

I would have liked to say farewell to the fans properly, but I'm sure they knew what I felt about them – and vice-versa. Having done so well since returning to the side, Branfoot then made it clear he wanted me to stay and sign a new contract, although whether he ever took me off the transfer list I'm not too sure to this day. Because I was coming to the end of my contract, Southampton

...illsborough School team photo, 1979, with me in the front row (skipper), minus ...ots but sporting the 'trendy' seventies hair-do of my idol Kevin Keegan.

...s on tour. I know it looks like I'm enjoying a typical lads' holiday. But it's actually ...England Under-19 squad in Brazil, 1987.

The Millwall squad (I'm standing third from right, back row) which took the old First Division by storm at the start of the 1988/89 season.

I enjoyed probably the happiest times of my career down on the south coast with Southampton.

Hurlock, a saint? Surely not. Terry taught me that 100 per cent effort was not enough.

Above: I know he got stung with a bung, but George Graham did me proud as my first 'agent'.

Right: The papers called him everything from 'Fash the Bash' to 'Fash the Cash', but John Fashanu will always be 'Fash the Flash' to me.

The style, the poise, the power, the concentration. Can you believe I only played once for England?

Pretty useful in the air, too! The fans at The Dell loved my aggressive approach and I loved them.

They called Terry Venables and Alan Sugar Tottenham's 'dream ticket' – but it turned out to be a nightmare for one of the greatest men in football.

I thought my diet was bad – but a Big Mac and fries as a pre-match meal, come on Matt.

No-one's safe when the Razor's at full pelt; not even my team-mates. Just as Gary Mabbutt.

Just the ticket! Paul Walsh, me, David Howells, Terry Fenwick and Tony Parks took Tottenham trips abroad seriously. Honest!

My lone protest against El Tel's sacking went down well with the Spurs' fans. Not with Alan Sugar.

A proud moment for me as I make my only full England appearance, against Nigeria at Wembley in November 1994.

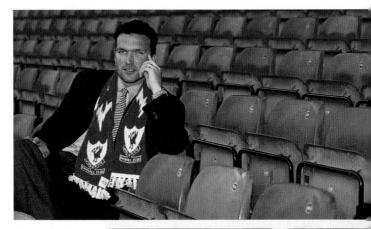

Above: Alan Sugar is history and I'm a Liverpool player now. Do I look smug or what?

Right: Graeme Souness (with Ronnie Moran and Phil Boersma) would have made Liverpool great again.

I took a nasty blow on the head scoring this late equaliser against Man United. Some say I never recovered.

'Beauty and the Beast' … that's me and my old Millwall mate, Teddy Sheringham. I'll let you decide who's who.

'Sacre Bleu'. Dear old Eric didn't like having his turned-up collar felt one little bit. So I did it again … and again …

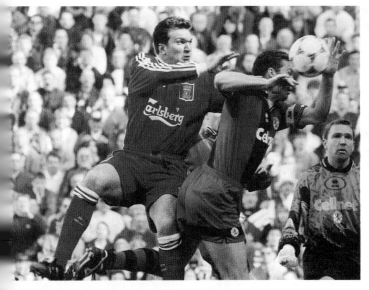

Former Middlesbrough skipper Nigel Pearson makes a brave attempt to stop me getting a goal-bound header, but goalkeeper Alan Miller (bottom right) thinks better of it.

Party time! The drinks flowed after winning the League Cup with Liverpool in 1995. And it wasn't Coca Cola!

Above: Conclusive proof that me and Alan Shearer really *are* the best of mates.

Right: Not the most flattering photo in the world as Jamie Redknapp and I savour Wembley success.

knew that they wouldn't get the price they wanted if the transfer went to a tribunal, and they also knew that it would cost them a lot of money to replace me with a player of similar quality. They should have thought about that earlier, rather than dumping me in the reserves and making me train with the kids as punishment for one moment of madness. I deserved better than that, as most Southampton fans will tell you. But despite the club's efforts to persuade me to extend my stay on the South Coast, I felt it was time to move on. My mind was made up and I'd set my heart on a return to White Hart Lane once it became clear that my old club and my old boss wanted me back. I had some great times down at The Dell and I will never forget the way so many people accepted me and made the majority of my spell down on the South Coast such a happy one. The family had a great life down there and made many friends whom we still keep in touch with. But it was time to move on and once I knew that Terry Venables was serious about taking me back to Tottenham, there was no turning back. I had some unfinished business to attend to at White Hart Lane. There were other clubs interested in me at the time – Sheffield Wednesday and Nottingham Forest – but the opportunity to work with Terry again was too inviting to turn down because I rated him as the best coach in the business, and still do. He was great for me because he knew me as a player and a person inside out. Terry reminded me of the conversation we'd had when he sold me to Southampton; how sometimes you have to step down to come back up and that was exactly how things had worked out. I was out of contract at Southampton and met up with Terry at a hotel in Kensington, London during the summer before he went away on holiday. He told me that he wanted me to sign for Spurs and said 'Don't do anything while I'm away' so I bided my time until he returned and everything went through as planned. Well, almost. I was really excited about the prospect of going back to such a great club, but I did have an anxious wait for the deal to go through because the clubs could not agree on a fee and the transfer had to be settled by the old tribunal system. Southampton valued me at £1.5 million whereas Tottenham were only prepared to offer £400,000 (cheers, Tel) so in the end they settled on £750,000 and I was a Tottenham player again. And not just any old player either, because Terry Venables paid me the ultimate compliment by making me captain at the start of the 1993–94 season. In addition to that, I was also given the number six shirt (in the days before we had squad numbers) which was also flattering because that was the number the great Dave Mackay wore as skipper in Tottenham's halcyon days. It was totally unexpected but a major confidence-booster after everything that had gone on, and further proof that the manager had faith in both my ability and my leadership qualities.

He even sought my advice when he was on the look-out for a new striker that season, and he couldn't decide whether to go for Teddy Sheringham or John Fashanu. No disrespect to Fash but I didn't think he would have suited Spurs' style of play because he was so used to all the route one stuff he had played virtually throughout his career with Millwall and then Wimbledon. I told the boss 'You've got to buy Teddy', because he was such an intelligent footballer – a smashing player and one of the best I have played with – and I knew he would be good for Spurs. With that, the deal was done and just as I had predicted Teddy was a great success and slotted into the team perfectly from day one. Making me captain and seeking my opinion on such matters confirmed what I already knew about Terry; that he was a fantastic man-manager. I think that was his way of letting me know that he wasn't concerned about reputations, good or bad, and he obviously believed that the extra responsibility would have a calming influence on me. And it did, for two games at any rate!

Because that's how long it took me to pick up my first red card in a Tottenham shirt, although the manager was the first person to assure me I had been harshly treated by referee Phillip Don. I'd been 'P Don' from a great height, that's for sure!

I was involved in a little scuffle with Crystal Palace's Andy Thorn, nothing serious, and was sent packing. I couldn't believe it. Neither could Terry, who rushed down from his place in the main stand to meet me as I came off the field and reassure me that I was the unfortunate victim of another diabolical piece of refereeing. A red card three games into my new Tottenham career was hardly the start I needed, especially after telling all the papers what a changed man I was and how the Spurs captaincy would bring the best, not the beast, out in me. Needless to say, the papers had a field day, suggesting I'd learned nothing from my experiences at Southampton and suddenly I was branded the villain again. Which, on this occasion at least, simply wasn't justified, as Terry went to great lengths to point out after the game. It was a nothing incident and if it had been any other Spurs player, I doubt whether it would even have merited a booking let alone a sending off. But, because it was me and because I'd returned to White Hart Lane with a bad reputation – 'the dirtiest player in football' one magazine or newspaper had labelled me – the referee chose to make an issue of it and give me the red card.

It was desperately frustrating because I honestly had been working hard to clean up my act, going to great lengths to assure the media and the game's authorities that 'my mad days' were over. I remember saying at the time that it takes three seconds to get a reputation and about three years to get rid of it. I certainly wasn't the crazy man some people made me out to be and the arrival of my two children, Josh and Millie, had certainly helped to calm me down.

I'm the first to admit that I've made a few mistakes, but to read some stories you would think that I spent most of my spare time boozing, brawling and betting. Sure, I liked a drink and a flutter on the horses – still do – but the reputation I had been landed with was both unfair and unjust. Having gone through such a depressing time when I thought I'd blown everything, I had learned my lesson and was desperate to make amends second time around at Spurs; especially after being named skipper in the absence of Gary Mabbutt. That's why I was so heartbroken about being sent off against Palace so soon after my move.

Terry assured me I hadn't let myself or the club down, even though the press were straight on my back after the game, and that he would stand by me, whatever the criticism – which was exactly the sort of reaction I didn't get from Ian Branfoot the previous season. But that was typical of Terry, who would support his players no matter what, which was why he was held in such high esteem by everyone in the squad. Particularly by me.

It was as a result of that incident against Palace that Terry came out with the sort of classic, witty comment which he has become renowned for. I can recall it as if it were yesterday how Terry confronted Mr Don and, with more than a hint of sarcasm in his voice, asked the offending official: 'Referee, if I call you a w*****, will I be in trouble?' 'Yes'. 'What if I thought you were a w*****?' 'No'. 'In that case, I think you're a w*****.' Priceless. It was almost worth getting sent off to hear that and we still laugh about it when we meet up nowadays. Being suspended so early in the season was no laughing matter, however.

Terry put me straight back in the team afterwards though and I played in virtually every game from then on. I picked up a few bookings here and there, but nothing serious and only to be expected when you are a defender who is totally committed in every game, who wants to win every tackle. That's the way I am. I'd tried to cut out the silly stuff – arguing with refs and getting involved in soppy scuffles – but I couldn't change the way I played the game. Terry didn't want that. He took me back to Spurs to add some steel to the side and I'd like to think I did that. The Tottenham fans seemed to appreciate my efforts and that counts for a lot in my book. In fact I have always got on with the supporters at every club I've played for because they see me as a whole-hearted player who is always prepared to stand up and be counted.

Ironically, my first league game for Spurs on my return was away at Southampton and I got a great reception from the fans down there who appreciated my reasons for leaving and went out of their way to let me know they didn't hold it against me. If anything they were more angry with the club and the management for forcing my hand. A 0–0 draw on the opening day was a satisfactory result all round and gave an early indication that Tel's new-look, young team meant business and we weren't a bunch of fanny merchants. The back four provided the platform for us to make a fairly solid start to the season and, with Teddy banging a few goals in up front, everything was looking rosy.

Young Ian Walker and Erik 'The Viking' Thorstvedt were sharing the goalkeeping duties that season whilst I was a regular fixture at the heart of the defence, playing alongside Jason Cundy to start with and later the magnificent Gary Mabbutt; a model professional. In addition, we had some wonderfully talented players in the squad with Darren Anderton and Nicky Barmby really beginning to make an impact, and Teddy enjoying what was arguably his best-ever season for the club. Teddy scored 28 goals that season but it wasn't just for his goals that he was so important to us; he made the whole team tick with his enthusiasm and intelligence and was the perfect player for the younger lads to look up to. Although we were never consistent enough, a long-standing Tottenham trait it seems, to make a serious assault for a European place via the league, we played some terrific stuff at times – and the team spirit was magnificent. With characters like Steve Sedgley, Vinny Samways – 'Vinegar Sandwich' – and David Howells – or 'Oliver Reed' as he was known for obvious reasons – there wasn't much danger of it being anything else. The joke doing the rounds was that Olly Reed died because he'd been out on a session with David.

'Sedge', in particular, was great for morale because he was one crazy guy who would do anything for a laugh, or to be the centre of attention. The club prankster. I can remember being woken up in the middle of the night, whilst in a hotel prior to an away game, by Steve who seemed to be crying out for help. I went to the door of my room at about 2 am and he was stood there without a stitch on, screaming in agony with something sticking out of each nostril. On closer inspection, it turned out that he'd got two wine gums hanging from his nose so I took him inside because he was causing such a scene and tried to remove the offending sweets. As we freed one he put it in his mouth and ate it, then did the same with the other (he also removed one from somewhere else, but we won't go into that) before saying 'thanks a lot' and returning to his room without a word of explanation. I later found out that he had actually ordered a 2 am wake-up call just so he could wind me up and ruin my sleep. Strange boy, 'Sedge'.

No-one was safe from his tomfoolery, not even opponents from our great North London rivals Arsenal. Just ask Paul Merson, who was driving home from training with his club as me and Steve were making our way back from the Tottenham training ground. When 'Sedge' saw Paul, he stripped off totally in the front seat before sprinting down the road after Merse's car, tapped on his window and then carried on running across the traffic lights before sitting on a bollard, waving to the bemused Arsenal striker. Paul was in hysterics, and it's little wonder he turned to drink. You needed one whenever 'Sedge' was on the warpath. He wouldn't look out of place on the *Jerry Springer Show*. There are plenty of other wild stories I could tell about him, but his mum might be reading this book.

Talking of 'wild', they didn't come much wilder than

defender Pat Van den Hauwe who was the sort of character who was liable to explode at any minute – and invariably did. Light the blue touch paper and watch him go. He had the shortest temper in the world and I can remember him trying to get out of the Tottenham training ground one day via a huge metal gate which opened outwards as opposed to in.

Needless to say, when Pat tried to pull the gate open, it didn't budge and, needless to say, the big man went mad as he yanked at the metal exit which he virtually removed from its hinges before walking out in a rage to a waiting car. Much to the amusement of passers-by. But that was Pat for you, and you just never knew from one day to the next what sort of mood he was going to be in; or whether he would actually bother coming into training at all. We nicknamed him 'Reggie' (Perrin) with very good reason because he would go AWOL for days on end without any explanation; missing, presumed dead. Then he would suddenly reappear and get on with his work as if nothing happened, and no-one ever dared question his actions. He was a law unto himself. He had his rules and if you didn't like them, tough. Pat had those dangerous eyes which told you what sort of mood he was in, and I can remember trying to have a crack with him one day and he just stared at me and said: 'Don't wind me up, Razor; don't get me at it.' Enough said. I think even the managers he played for were scared of him, or wary of him, and he got away with things other players wouldn't. He didn't really mix with the lads at all, and he would either go missing for a few days or go home to his wife, the model Mandy Smith. A little unreliable and unpredictable, but still a good player, which is what you had to be to play for Terry Venables.

Playing alongside players of such quality helped me find a good level of consistency, as was indicated by the number of man of the match awards I was picking up, and after a few months I was suddenly being talked about as an England contender which made a pleasant change from being called a thug. But that just goes to show how fickle football folk – whether they are fans, management or media – can be. It was nice to get some decent publicity for a change and a bit of recognition for my ability and, looking back, that was probably one of the best seasons of my career in terms of consistency. I played 38 games in the league alone that season which I consider good value-for-money, and even managed to chip in with a few important goals against Leeds, Liverpool and an absolute screamer against Norwich. It was a very exciting time because the new team was gelling, we were playing entertaining football and, for the second season running, I was on the Wembley trail again.

The FA Cup run really began to gather momentum when we beat Wimbledon, as we had done in my first spell with Spurs, in the Fifth Round with yours truly once again getting rave reviews for my performance. The fact I was up against my old mate John Fashanu and hardly gave him a kick made the 3–2 win at White Hart Lane all the more satisfying. There was no love lost between the two teams and it was always going to be a battle against the likes of Vinnie Jones and Fash, but we were up for it and probably surprised a few people with our resolve and character.

Wimbledon had been wound up in the build-up to the game by the comments of 'Mr Squeaky Clean' Gary Lineker, a great favourite with the Tottenham fans during his spell there, when he said on television that the best place to watch Wimbledon was on Ceefax. Not like Gary to be controversial but it certainly struck a nerve with manager Joe Kinnear and his boys, and gave our fans good cause to chant Lineker's name once again.

After beating Manchester City in the quarter-finals it was on to Wembley for a North London showdown with Arsenal and, as you can imagine, there was an enormous amount of pride, as well as prestige, at stake there. It was a frustrating occasion because two crucial decisions, one at either end of the field, ultimately decided the game, in their favour. For starters, we had a clear-cut penalty turned down early in the game when Andy Linighan sent Darren Anderton sprawling in the box, yet nothing was given. It was one of the most blatant penalties you will see and the decision by the officials was, quite frankly, embarrassing. Arsenal's winning goal was also a red-face affair for our keeper Erik Thorstvedt who had been brilliant all season but whose crucial error of judgement cost us our place in the final. The Gunners had a free-kick well outside the area and Erik asked for four players in the wall when we really only needed two. Arsenal packed our area and we were under-manned at the back, with the result that Tony Adams stole in to score with a simple header at the far post with about ten minutes remaining.

Apart from the disappointment of losing an FA Cup semi-final to our greatest rivals, I would say it was a successful season for the club; certainly for me. That summer Terry was looking to strengthen the squad still further and the club really looked to have a bright future; until Mr Sugar went to war with the greatest coach in the country and denied Tel the opportunity to turn his beloved Spurs into a recognised force once more. That was his dream – and ours – but it was about to be destroyed.

CHAPTER SEVEN

Sugar Turned Everything Sour

With a successful and encouraging 1992–93 season coming to a close and just the FA Cup final between Arsenal and Sheffield Wednesday to go, a number of the Tottenham lads, myself included, headed off to the Football Writers' Player of the Year dinner in great spirits. We'd had a good year, proved a lot of people wrong (I certainly had) and we were happy in the knowledge that the club was on a sound footing, with the best coach in the business at the helm. With the addition of a few new players, to complement the likes of myself, Teddy Sheringham, Darren Anderton and Nick Barmby who had all performed so well, there was no reason why we couldn't turn a top ten position in the league into a top six, or even higher, next season. Either way the future looked promising, the club was buzzing and we were going to enjoy our summer break, starting with the Football Writers' Dinner at the Royal

Lancaster Hotel in London's West End. Or so we thought.

What started out as a great evening turned into an absolute disaster that we could never have imagined. The shock announcement that Terry Venables was parting company with his beloved Spurs, the club he had committed so much time, effort and personal wealth to, ruined the night, the summer and, effectively, changed the course of my career once more. We were devastated when we heard the news. Some of the lads were close to tears and I don't mind admitting that I was one of them.

The first I knew of impending events was when my agent Eric Hall, a long-time friend of Terry's, came to see me, Teddy Sheringham and David Howells and said, in typical straight-to-the-point fashion, 'Tel's getting the sack tomorrow'. We were gobsmacked and not sure, initially, if Eric was having a wind-up. After all, we'd just beaten our great rivals Arsenal 3–0, finished the season well and everything was moving in the right direction. Why the hell should the manager get the sack? It didn't make any sense. But when we went upstairs to see Terry himself, he confirmed the news that he was on his way. He was nearly in tears, too. Our initial reaction was, 'If you're going, then we're going', but Tel told us not to do anything rash and kept saying, 'Don't worry, you'll be alright'. But without him, it just wasn't going to be the same. Terry Venables *was* Tottenham Hotspur.

The bottom line was that he couldn't get on with Chairman Alan Sugar and he couldn't see a way to resolve their differences. He explained that there would be a big announcement the next day, the Friday, and advised us not to say anything to anyone or do anything until it was out in the open. But he wanted the players to hear it from him personally, rather than through a statement from the club, which was typical of the relationship we had with Terry.

No-one knew that anything was going on behind the scenes and there had certainly been no indication that Sugar was going to boot Terry out, but on the Friday before the Cup final came confirmation that the chairman had called a meeting of the directors to have Terry voted off the board and sacked as chief executive. That was when it all began to sink in and the players and all the staff were in complete shock; it was like someone had shot your leg off. Everyone loved Terry and a phrase we used at the time summed up the spirit he had created and the respect we had for him.

'When one of us gets kicked, we all limp'.

We were all in it together. I couldn't see myself playing for any other manager at Spurs. When Tel got kicked, I limped for him and carried on limping long after some of the others had stopped. But when we first heard the news, all the players were right behind him and agreed we would stick by him no matter what. I think it was the relationship he had with everyone at White Hart Lane, the fact that he was so popular, that really got up Sugar's nose. He couldn't seem to stand the fact that Terry was liked while he was feared and generally disliked. It was obvious too that the chairman didn't like some of the people Terry, in his position as chief executive, had brought on board, people like his personal assistant Eddie Ashby.

From the players' point of view, we didn't see why personality clashes at board level should be allowed to affect the whole club and undermine what the players and Terry in particular were trying to achieve on the field. Surely Sugar could see the progress the team had been making and, as far as the financial side of things were concerned, the club was in a much better state than before the two of them had joined forces as the so-called 'dream ticket' to put Spurs back up there with the big boys. That was where we were heading, at least we thought we were, but this bitter personal conflict altered everything, and all the proposed changes Terry had planned in order to strengthen the squad during that summer went on hold. The club missed out on signing quality players like Tim Flowers, Roy Keane, Les Ferdinand and Des Walker; and I missed out on a lucrative five-year deal Terry had promised me once the season was over. The whole thing was a mess and suddenly Spurs, having restored at least some pride at a time when Arsenal were ruling the roost down the road, were a laughing stock again.

Verbally, Terry and I had agreed a new contract, which had been the arrangement when I signed my original, four-year deal on returning to White Hart Lane. He said at the time that, if I had a good season and improved my discipline, he would review the deal and pay me accordingly. And I knew that he would be every bit as good as his word. I trusted him implicitly. But before we had managed to put pen to paper, Sugar went to war and Terry was out. As a result, my career, my future was up in the air too. Other players were equally angry, concerned and unsettled by the events and I can recall David Howells, for one, coming out and saying in the press that he didn't want to play for Spurs without Venables and that Sugar had 'killed the club' by getting rid of him. Ask any Tottenham fan today about the team Terry was building and they will tell you it was the best they'd had for years and would have gone on to challenge for the major honours within the next year or two. It was essentially a young team and one which should have been kept together, and developed, at all costs.

The players felt strongly about the whole affair and were 100 per cent behind Terry as he fought through the courts to be reinstated, so much so that we immediately called a team meeting – at the aptly named 'Thank God It's Friday' restaurant near the club's Mill Hill training ground – to discuss what actions, if any, we would take. We agreed that we would be united in our support for Terry and show Sugar that we meant business. However, as the affair dragged on, I was the only one who stuck to my guns and it became something of a one-man crusade in the end as the other lads gave up the fight. I had put in a transfer request straightaway, that's how strongly I felt about the whole situation, but the others got cold feet and became increasingly worried about their own futures at the club. My suspicion was that Sugar had got to them and must have put pressure on the lads to cool their protest and effectively side with him, or else! The players didn't say as much, but their attitude changed once the whole squad had been summoned to a meeting with Sugar which he held in my absence as I was unable to attend.

I don't know exactly what was said at that meeting, but the essence of it was that the players were under contract and, as such, had a responsibility to the club and not just the manager. Sugar must have laid down the law pretty firmly, because everyone went quiet after that meeting, which disappointed me because we'd all agreed we would stick together on this one. There was no way I was backing down now and I was determined to see it through to the bitter end. I wasn't worried what action the chairman might take because, having had such a good season, I was confident that I'd get a move to another big club. (Bigger, as it turned out.) So while the lads maintained a diplomatic silence after their meeting with Sugar, I went on the radio, *5 Live* I think it was, to voice my disgust, having already been pictured in the papers on the Friday before the Cup final at a testimonial match for a popular, former Tottenham player called Eddie Baily at Enfield, parading a banner with 'VENABLES MUST STAY – WITHOUT SUGAR' in front of approving Tottenham fans. Not to be outdone, my wife Sarah took the protest a step further by staging her own demonstration, with placards and everything, outside Sugar's home in Chigwell. As I said earlier in the book: take on one Ruddock, you take on all of us. I obviously realised that our public stand against the chairman was probably not the greatest career move I'd ever made, but that was how strongly we both felt. It certainly endeared me to the Spurs supporters at the time, although some of them did turn against me later and call me 'Judas' when I eventually moved on to Liverpool for the sort of big bucks I'd been promised by Terry but denied by Sugar.

I put in a transfer request because I wasn't prepared to accept the way I had been treated and Sugar didn't like that either. He wasn't used to people turning him down or questioning his decisions; he was surrounded by 'yes' men and didn't appear to know the meaning of the word 'no'.

The situation came to a head during the summer, after I'd made my feelings perfectly clear to all and sundry, when Sugar phoned me at a hotel in Portugal to discuss my future. By this time it was pretty clear that Terry would not be coming back to Spurs but, even though I'd been the major spokesman for the players over his sacking, I was still prepared to stay at the club. Of course, I was sorry to see Terry go, but I loved the club and would have stayed ... if they had been prepared to pay me what I was prom-ised. And after what was a fairly amicable conversation with the chairman from my holiday hotel, I got the distinct impression he would honour Tel's verbal agreement. He even said he would look into the matter of compensating me for the £50,000 it had cost me on out-of-pocket expenses when I moved back to London from Southampton, although he later denied making any such assurances or promises. I told him what I wanted and he said, 'I'll see what I can do', and it seemed he was prepared to bury the hatchet and offer me a new deal which would make me a Spurs player until I was 31. Who knows, I might even have been a Tottenham player for life; that's what I was suddenly thinking after the dust had settled. Sugar told me to put my requests in writing and we would discuss things when I returned from holiday.

The day after flying back from the Algarve I went to his beautiful home in Chigwell, Essex and it was then he insisted he had 'agreed to nothing'. Soon after, at his Amstrad offices in Brentwood, he told me he had taped the conversation we'd had while I was out in Portugal. I was stunned by the whole situation. It was becoming clear that he was trying to force me into a corner, which shouldn't have surprised me considering his reputation as a ruthless businessman and negotiator. I couldn't believe he'd actually taped our phone conversation and when Sugar then produced a tape with a recording of a 'private and confidential' conversation he'd had with Terry, about me, I was absolutely astonished. Needless to say, Terry was also furious when I told him that the chairman, his business partner, was taping conversations and playing them to people without his knowledge.

It was all getting out of hand and made me increasingly suspicious of Sugar who, by now, had appointed Ossie Ardiles as the club's new manager. I didn't rant and rave out of respect for the chairman, my boss, but I never once got the same respect in return and from then on it was always going to be difficult to bridge the gap, gulf more like, that existed between us. I couldn't see how I could ever be happy playing for the club while he was still in charge, even though the new manager was a great hero of mine, having played with him briefly during my first spell at the club. I was only 19 at the time but Ossie treated me brilliantly, took me under his wing if you like, and became my room-mate and a good friend. He attended a party to celebrate my engagement to Sarah and even got up on stage to sing a song. I couldn't believe it at the time; the great Ossie Ardiles, World Cup winner, singing at my engagement party. I had a lot of respect for him and he was one of the very few people the fans would have accepted as a replacement for Terry. I explained to Ossie about the contract situation and the arrangement I had with Terry and, in his very distinctive voice, he said, 'Don't worry, I will sort something out'. As he was such a high-profile figure brought in by Sugar to reunite the players, I thought he would carry some weight when it came to contractual matters, but it soon became clear that he wouldn't have the ultimate say. Sugar still held all the cards and controlled the finances. In the middle of the meeting at the chairman's house, after I'd discussed my situation with Ossie, he went out into another room with Sugar and director Tony Berry whilst I went for a walk around the garden, convinced everything would soon be settled and that Ossie would get me what I wanted. But after a short while the three of them returned and turned me down flat. There was no discussion or negotiation; the deal remained the same.

If the club had been prepared to bend a little bit, I'm sure we could have come to a compromise and I might well have still been a Spurs player today. But Sugar wasn't budging. I was earning around £1500 a week at the time and I knew for a fact that the top salary amongst the playing staff at White Hart Lane was double that. I believed, especially having been skipper for a while that season, that I deserved to be on the same sort of money as the top-earners at the club.

As far as I was concerned it was a simple situation, but it was all getting out of hand and by now I just didn't know where I stood, especially as Ossie couldn't seem to make up his mind whether he wanted me or not. One day he was saying I could leave and that he wouldn't stand in my way; the next he was telling the press we were still in negotiations and that he was doing everything he could to keep me at the club. Frankly I was finding it all very confusing and it was hard to know what Sugar wanted out of all of this as well. I received a copy of a letter which Sugar had sent to the club secretary Peter Barnes, asking if he could find out what terms I'd been offered by Venables in order to 'pacify Mr Ruddock if the Board feels that the terms are favourable'.

He also said in the same letter that the club would do

its 'utmost' to make sure I was happy at Spurs, before going on to tell Mr Barnes to find out which part of the country I would like to move to. It was all getting too bizarre for words, but the saga took another incredible twist before I eventually signed on the dotted line for Liverpool.

Although my mind was in turmoil, and my family life had been turned upside down, I was in the fortunate position of knowing that a number of top clubs and big-name managers had made inquiries about me. There was Graeme Souness at Liverpool, Kenny Dalglish at Blackburn, Kevin Keegan at Newcastle and Glenn Hoddle at Chelsea. Not a bad little selection. Then totally out of the blue, and at a time when my agent Eric Hall was already in negotiations with Blackburn and Liverpool, Ossie indicated that Spurs were actually prepared to offer me what I wanted after all. What a ludicrous state of affairs. I don't know if it was the stress of the whole situation that caused it, but I was laid low with a stomach bug and unable to travel with the Spurs squad on a pre-season trip to Ireland. Not that I was too keen on going anyway, given the situation I was in at the time. Sarah phoned to tell people at the club I was ill and couldn't travel but they obviously didn't believe the story as Spurs insisted on sending a club doctor round (yet again!) to check on my condition. He even prescribed medication for me.

Then things started to get really messy as, right at the point I was prepared to commit myself to Liverpool, the club I had chosen to join because of the influence of Graeme Souness, Spurs tried to block the move by refusing to send the registration forms because of yet another dispute over money. Tottenham had owed me a signing-on fee which had been due the previous month and, although they eventually agreed to cough up the cash, they then started quibbling about two other sets of fees I would have been entitled to if I had stayed at the club for the duration of my contract. The powers-that-be at Spurs wouldn't release my forms to Liverpool until I had signed an agreement waiving any rights to those payments. On top of that, I was then required to sign another letter agreeing not to talk to the press about anything that had gone on at Spurs during this long, crazy summer. I was happy to sign everything they requested, because by now I had set my heart on a move to Liverpool and simply wanted to conclude the deal which was worth double what I was asking for at Spurs.

Even though they'd asked me not to go to the press, the day after I'd signed for Souness and Liverpool, Sugar and Ardiles slaughtered me in the papers, branding me greedy and a trouble-maker. As a result, the Tottenham fans who had backed me throughout this whole, sorry affair turned against me and in addition to receiving hate mail from hundreds of Spurs supporters, I was slaughtered and called 'Judas' the next time I went back to White Hart Lane. That hurt. The comments and criticism from Sugar I could handle because, as far as I'm concerned, his views are worth nothing.

But for Ossie, someone I considered a friend as well as an idol, to come out and say the things he did, now that did upset me. He later phoned me at my hotel in Liverpool to say how sorry he was that the fans had abused me, but I let my wife Sarah take the call as I'd lost respect for him. Even though we shook hands after we'd played against Spurs at Anfield, I couldn't forget what he had done and knew the old friendship would never be the same again.

As for my relationship with Sugar, that continued to go downhill and all the old feelings were stirred up again a couple of years later when, during an interview with the *Sunday Mirror*, I was asked what I thought about the way he ran the club, and of Spurs' prospects for the future. I went on record at the time as saying, 'Tottenham will never be anything while Sugar is in charge'. That was my honest view then and I stand by those comments although now, with my old boss George Graham running the football side of things, you wouldn't rule out the prospect of the glory days returning to White Hart Lane.

Needless to say, Sugar wasn't prepared to let my comments go without hitting back and he made an official complaint to the Football Association about me and I was suddenly facing a charge of bringing the game into disrepute. After all the things Sugar had said about me, there was no way I was going to take my punishment lying down, so I applied for a personal hearing which never actually materialised because, in the meantime, we had acquired through the *Sun* newspaper archives more than thirty derogatory comments Sugar had made about me. I think the FA realised this had the makings of another soap opera, so they decided to drop the charges against me, much to Sugar's disgust I'm sure. Another victory to Ruddock! I shouldn't really hold anything against him because, without Mr Alan Sugar, I would not have had the opportunity to play for one of the most glamorous clubs in the country. But I was still deeply saddened by what had happened during that traumatic summer. I felt for Terry and I felt for the fans whose hopes and dreams for the new season had been shattered. Even at the time, I sensed that the heart had been ripped out of the club and that the wounds would take ages, years, to heal. From what people tell me, the club hasn't been the same since. The atmosphere, the camaraderie, the passion within the club had been destroyed.

Terry had turned Tottenham into a warm, family club, yet one with determination and ambition. His departure was a tremendous blow to the club and was felt by all the players. In my opinion, the club would be in a damn sight healthier position nowadays if Terry had been allowed to finish what he started. Show me a sane Tottenham fan, most of whom have forgiven me now, I'm pleased to say, who thinks otherwise.

CHAPTER EIGHT

The Rock of Anfield

After all the dreadful dealings with Alan Sugar and Co. throughout the summer of 1993, it was a total relief to finally have my future sorted out and my mind put at rest. Manager Graeme Souness, chairman David Moores and chief executive Peter Robinson were thoroughly professional and totally straight.

Apart from the problems over the release of the registration papers by Spurs, the negotiations with Liverpool went like a dream and from the first moment I met the management team, I knew Anfield was the place for me. There was no quibbling over terms and my agent Eric 'Monster, Monster' Hall hardly needed to call on his rather unique bargaining skills, shall we call them. He always used to say, 'I make the poor players rich, and the rich players richer' and I was certainly happy with the deal Liverpool put on the table, especially after struggling to get an extra grand or so out of Spurs.

Not that money was the only consideration, you understand. There had been no shortage of offers and, having already had talks with Kenny Dalglish's number two at Blackburn, Ray Harford, I'd intended to hear what Glenn Hoddle and Chelsea had to say before meeting Kevin Keegan to talk about a possible move to Newcastle. But once I'd spoken to the people at Liverpool, Graeme Souness in particular, my mind was made up. I'd always admired and respected Souness as a player – so skilful, yet so committed – and I just had this feeling that he would be my kind of manager. Like Terry Venables, in many ways. It was a great thrill for me to be signing for a club with such a magnificent tradition, especially as they'd paid a then record fee, £2.5 million, for a defender. And you couldn't fail to be impressed with the set-up at Anfield. The Liverpool players were a great bunch of lads too, as I was quickly to find out.

On the day I signed, I met up with Jamie Redknapp and Steve McManaman at the hotel where I was staying and, after a quick introduction, we went off into town to meet up with some of my other Liverpool team-mates. We ended up in a bar singing on the karaoke and after a quick rendition of 'Strangers In The Night' I was soon accepted as one of the boys. The fans who had seen the story about me signing in the local paper, or heard the news on the radio, seemed to take to me as well and I remember thinking, 'What a start to my Liverpool career this is'. The next day, following my first training session, I learned that the boys were playing in a golf tournament at Royal Birkdale so that gave me another ideal opportunity to get to know a few more of the lads in a relaxed environment. After a round of golf, we all went into town for a night out, capped by Don Hutchison's infamous Budweiser trick which made the inside pages of the *News of the World* a few days later. There were a few girls celebrating the fact they were going to

University and, as they were recording the occasion on video camera, the temptation for an exhibitionist like 'Hutch' was too much to ignore.

As the camera panned round, there he was with his trousers and boxers down by his ankles and a Budweiser label strategically placed on his 'old man'. It was hilarious and everyone took it in good spirit, even the parents of the girls who got an eyeful, but the stunt landed Hutch in a spot of bother when the papers got hold of some stills and displayed them to the world. It was really only a harmless stunt, a giggle, but Hutch was called everything from a prat to a pervert in the press. At the time, no-one was offended, but afterwards someone obviously sensed that they could make a few quid by selling it to the papers and suddenly Don's tackle was the talk of the town. I don't know what all the fuss was about, because the label covered it all anyway! Welcome to Liverpool FC, Razor! I know what it's like to be labelled a 'bad boy' and that's really what happened to Don who was suddenly stuck with a reputation of being something of a hell-raiser himself. He was certainly a fiery character on the field who enjoyed the *craic* off it, but some of the stick he took over that was diabolical. It certainly didn't do him any favours and it wasn't too long before Hutch was on his way to West Ham; a move I was to make a few years later.

From that moment on, I had a funny feeling that my spell on Merseyside was going to be incident-packed and it wasn't long before I was the one making the news for all the wrong reasons. I hadn't even played a league game for the club when I hit the headlines for what I swear to this day was an accidental clash with Peter Beardsley which left the former Liverpool favourite with a fractured cheek-bone. It was my first game at Anfield for my new club and Peter was playing for Newcastle at the time in a testimonial match for Ronnie Whelan. The game was only ten minutes old when he went to flick-on an aerial ball and his face collided with my shoulder as I came in to challenge. No foul was given, there was no reaction from the Newcastle players who were close to the incident and video evidence failed to suggest that the challenge was illegal. I certainly never set out to hurt him, and was shocked to see him so seriously injured, but that didn't stop him trying to sue me for loss of earnings. He also wrote in his autobiography that I deliberately broke his cheek-bone to prove to the Kop early on in my Liverpool career that I was a hard man, so we sued the newspaper which ran the serialisation and I came away with £10,000 for my troubles.

I was disappointed he felt the need to take such a course of action, and then try and make me out to be a bully in his book, because blaming a fellow-professional for deliberately setting out to hurt you is a very serious accusation to make. I knew in my own mind that there was no intent and I think, deep down, Peter knew that was the case too. I think he was poorly advised by the people close to him (allegedly, his wife!) because that sort of incident should never end up in court. I was never charged with anything so my conscience was clear. Even so, the papers made me out to be the villain yet again and the reputation I'd got at Southampton after the head-butt incident with Craig Short came to the surface once more.

Graeme Souness, like Terry Venables after I'd been sent off playing for Spurs against Crystal Palace the previous season, was quick to jump to my defence and point out that a free-kick wasn't even awarded against me, so how could I be accused of malice? It was nonsense and, as 'Souey' said at the time, it was simply a case of my reputation going before me. If anything, the slight re-arrangement of his face did Pete a favour! A year later, after all the sueing and counter-sueing had finished, we were in the England squad together and I think he was more embarrassed than me about it all. He was really nice to me after that.

Quite an eventful introduction to my Liverpool career then, and I was pleased to get a win under my belt in my first league game against Sheffield Wednesday, which we won 2–0 thanks to a couple of goals from Nigel Clough, who was making his debut for the club at the same time. He scored a screamer in the first half and I set up his second with a header which Chris Woods could only parry, in front of the Kop too, so I couldn't have asked for a better start. I was pleased for Nigel ('the young man', as we used to call the son of Brian) because he was under a bit of pressure to produce the goods after his move from Nottingham Forest. He was a nice lad, not exactly one of the boys because he didn't drink or get involved in any of the silly stuff, but a clever fella who was always handy to have around when we were struggling with the crossword on the team bus. We used to shout the questions out and he'd be back with the answer, quick as a flash.

Nigel was also on target in the next game, a 3–1 win at QPR, and he looked tailor-made for a Liverpool side playing such positive, open football. He was renowned for his intelligent play, both in terms of his use of the ball and the runs he made off it, and I thought he would go on to be a Liverpool and England great. But his Anfield career never lived up to its early promise and after Souey left, he never seemed to get much of a look-in. The fact that Robbie Fowler had just burst onto the scene and was scoring goals alongside Ian Rush didn't help Cloughie's cause and I find it amazing that he never really achieved much as a player from then on. I hope he has better luck in management.

You certainly couldn't fault him in those early days at the club though, and I got off to a great start too, scoring my first league goal for Liverpool in the 5–0 thrashing of Swindon to put us top of the table. Three wins and only one goal conceded in our first three games was just the start we wanted, although the run came to an end a few days later when my old club Spurs turned us over at Anfield. But, all in all, I'd settled in pretty quickly and I think the year I'd had at Spurs, another massive club, helped me adjust quickly to life as a high-profile player with a top club after four, relatively low-key years with Southampton.

It was great to be part of a club which had such an incredible following all over the world and even now, when I'm on my travels, people still remember me as a Liverpool player. The fans took to me from the outset and I think that helped too. They could see what a whole-hearted player I was and it was nice when former Anfield legends like Tommy Smith, one of the game's genuine hard men in his day, used to say in his newspaper column that I was just the sort of defender Liverpool had been lacking over the years.

Tommy said I was worthy of his old title, the 'Anfield Iron Man' and one paper also flattered me with the headline 'RUDDOCK, THE ROCK OF ANFIELD' after I'd played my part in an impressive 2–0 win over Leeds in that first season. Tommy was still a big personality in the area and his columns were renowned for either caning people or loving them. Thankfully, he loved me and he often used to write that I was ready for the England side and would add some steel to the national team too, which was always nice to hear. It certainly made a change from all the crap I'd had to put up with from time to time.

Having said that, controversy was never far away and a couple of weeks later my name was being dragged through the mud again when I was accused of throwing a punch during a 1–0 defeat by Blackburn. There had been a bit of a scuffle, but I never threw a punch. To this day, I don't know the identity of the person who kicked up a fuss. It was certainly not Mike Newell, the player in question, who lived near me at the time and actually gave me a lift home after the game. But I still had to pay another visit to the FA who felt the need to hold an inquiry after someone had made a complaint about my alleged behaviour. The referee, Mike Reed, didn't even include it in his report and he made a point of coming up to me after I'd been cleared at the hearing to say that it wasn't anything to do with him, so it's anybody's guess who actually made the accusation. The thing is, if I had struck him, Mike would have known about it and there's every chance he would have gone down and the whole thing would have been seen by people in the ground, including the referee. As it was, I didn't even get booked but still had to attend a pointless hearing, and sit through a video of the incident which revealed nothing.

Once again, Souness was the first person to leap to my defence as he appealed to my critics to get off my back and give me a chance. He was happy with the way I was playing, and that was all that mattered to me. I seemed to carry on where I left off at Spurs, although I don't think I was as consistent as I had been during my year as skipper under Terry Venables at White Hart Lane. But the style of play Liverpool had made their trademark over the years certainly suited me because, contrary to the belief of some that I was just a stopper, I can actually play a bit too. I can knock it around with the best of them and I'd like to think I proved that during my time at Anfield. I laid on more balls than Joan Collins, as we used to say.

There was pressure on the guys at the back because the club had long been criticised for its defensive qualities, but with myself partnering Mark Wright in the middle of the back four, and with Rob Jones, David Burrows and later Julian Dicks playing at full-back, we had quite a formidable back line. No longer the pushovers people used to suggest. Wrighty was a great player, very much in the Alan Hansen mould, and after he began to pick up a few injuries the club bought John Scales and Phil Babb and we were one of the first teams to play with three at the back during the 1994–95 season. 'The triangle of bolsawood', as they used to call us.

There were a few others in the team, people like Ronnie Whelan and Jan Molby, who could look after themselves too, so we weren't a soft touch. Ronnie, in particular, was a right dirty so and so who gave as good as he got and knew when and where to put the boot in. He was an experienced pro who knew every trick in the book and had the medals to prove that more often than not, he was the man who came out on top. I remember going to 'The Legend's' house soon after my move to Anfield and his trophy cabinet was out of this world, packed with cups and honours he had won during a glittering career when Liverpool were at the top of the tree. I remember standing there in amazement and wondering whether I might one day boast a similar collection of awards. Maybe not.

Off the field too we were a hardy bunch, especially when it came to drinking and generally making the most of the high life. We worked hard but we played hard and that was a Liverpool trait long before I arrived at Anfield, going back to the days when manager Souness was a player and proudly carried the title 'Champagne Charlie'. I think one of the problems was that, as the manager, Souey obviously had to try and keep the players in check and I don't think the older pros who remembered him and what he was like from his days as a player – a man who loved the social aspect of being a professional footballer at a glamour club – took too kindly to him laying down the law. There were bad vibes between him and the senior players and I don't think the likes of Bruce Grobbelaar, John Barnes and Ronnie Whelan, people who had been around for years, gave Graeme the same respect as the newer members of the squad. There was lots of bickering and moaning behind his back and you could sense that not everyone was pulling in the same direction. The annoying thing was that no-one would confront the manager to his face; I don't think they dared. Instead, there were snide little comments being made here and there and the disharmony spilled over onto the pitch where some players were not performing to their full potential. Souey desperately wanted to be a success but without the total support of everyone in the squad, and with pressure mounting on him in the press, he decided to call it a day early in

1994 after we had lost in the FA Cup Third Round to Bristol City at home.

It's never easy when a player who is used to being 'one of the lads' and chief socialiser, like Souey, returns to a club and takes charge of players who used to be his team-mates. Suddenly, he was pulling them up for doing things he got away with as a strong-willed player and captain, the life and soul of the party, and it created an uneasy atmosphere at times. I think the older players resented him for laying down the law and felt he was being hypocritical. But you have different responsibilities when you are a manager and you have to distance yourself to a certain extent from the playing staff. Some of the players couldn't handle it. That's not to say Souey was aloof or unapproachable, but he wanted to do things his way. As manager he made a lot of changes, both in terms of personnel and the way the club was run, because he wanted to make the same mark at Anfield as he had done at Glasgow Rangers where success came easily to him.

He knew what he wanted and nothing was going to stand in his way, but when he failed to deliver the trophies people began to question his methods, and to suggest a return to the old Liverpool ways was the answer to the problem. Personally, I don't think it was and I honestly believe that, given time, Souness would have turned Liverpool into a major force once more. That was his dream. He wanted to be remembered as someone who made the club great as a player and even greater as a manager. He would have done too, if only he had been given the sort of time Alex Ferguson was allowed to get things right at Old Trafford. You look at what he has achieved at a club with similar resources and traditions and I believe that Souey, given the same sort of backing, could have been right up there alongside Sir Alex. We would have won the title within a couple of years if he had stayed, no doubt.

But he was taking more stick than he deserved and I think it all got too much for him, especially as he had undergone heart surgery a couple of years before and probably thought he didn't need all this hassle. In the end, he decided to go after the defeat by Bristol City which was a shame really because I loved working for the man and, after a dreadful run of five defeats in six games towards the end of August and throughout September, we'd improved in the league and had just enjoyed a magnificent result against Manchester United; coming back from three goals down to get a draw in a classic encounter at Anfield. I scored the equaliser about ten minutes from time, after Nigel Clough had pulled two goals back just before half-time, and I would love to say that I have great memories of that night. But I don't. I was quoted at the time as saying it was the greatest game I had ever played in, but the truth is I don't remember scoring the goal, celebrating it or playing out the last few minutes of what was a nail-biter, apparently.

That's because I suffered concussion when I powered in to score with a late header and clashed with another bone-head in Gary Pallister. I didn't know what was going on in those closing minutes and it wasn't until later, after I'd regained most of my senses, that I became fully aware of what I'd done. I also learned of a classic line Graeme Souness had produced off the cuff just after I'd scored the equaliser. I was still feeling groggy after lengthy treatment, not really knowing where I was, or who I was. Phil Boersma, the Liverpool physio at the time, returned to the dugout and relayed this information to the manager, saying: 'Razor says he doesn't know who he is.' At which point, the quick-witted Souness quipped: 'Well, in that case, get back out there and tell him he's f*****g Pele!' Sky TV wanted me to do an interview after the game but I couldn't oblige straightaway because I was too busy throwing up and nursing a wicked headache. Not that I minded too much once the lads told me what I'd done and I'd seen the goal on video later. People still talk about that game, and my goal in particular, because it was such an extraordinary comeback and I can recall Alex Ferguson saying in the papers the next day that he was absolutely furious because he'd never seen one of his sides blow a three-goal lead before.

It showed we had bottle, and we should really have used that result against a team more than ten points ahead of us in the league, as a springboard to better things. Instead we played like idiots against our next opponents, losing 1–0 at home to Bristol City, and Graeme was on his way. I was beginning to think I was some kind of jinx because in the space of 18 months I'd seen off two of the most respected managers in the game and, as was the case when Terry Venables was kicked out of Spurs, I was gutted when Souey left Liverpool. He was the man who bought me, he was the man I wanted to play for and I will always have the highest regard for him. I could see where he wanted to take the club, but those upstairs wanted success and they wanted it now, not later; especially with our arch-rivals Manchester United doing so well and already developing a real stranglehold on the Premiership.

But we had to put the disappointment and the shock

of Graeme's departure behind us and give the same sort of commitment to Roy Evans, who was rewarded for his remarkable service to the club as a player and a coach by being made manager of the club he loved. It was strange really, because one week we were calling him 'Eddie', his nickname for years, and beating him up on the training ground, and the next he was manager and we were calling him 'boss'. Souness left him a decent platform on which to build and the team wasn't far off Championship material; I was convinced of that at the time. How many sides could boast a forward line of Ian Rush, Robbie Fowler and John Barnes? This was the year Robbie began to make his mark and it was thanks to Souness that he was thrown into the side at such an early age. I remember watching a reserve game with Graeme who was keen to monitor the progress of this 'wonderkid' who was scoring goals galore in the second team. After the match, Souness was convinced Robbie could handle the step up to the first team and the boss turned to me and said at the time: 'The kid's ready; I've got to put him in the team.'

Sure enough, Robbie was given his chance and, boy, did he take it. After hitting six goals over two legs against Fulham in the Coca Cola Cup, he was soon scoring in the Premiership, and he served notice of what was to come with a stunning hat-trick in a 4–2 win over Southampton. I had the same feeling about Robbie's potential to go all the way as I'd had about Alan Shearer at The Dell. He is one of the best finishers I have ever seen, with either foot. I would put him on a par with the great Ian Rush and he was a much better natural finisher than Michael Owen, who was to follow him off the Anfield production line. Normally, young kids coming into the senior side need ten games or so to adapt to the pace and the extra pressure, but Robbie walked into the team and looked as though he'd been there for years. Everyone knew the kid was special and the frightening thing was that he was going to get better and better with experience. Robbie would be the first to acknowledge the part played by Ian Rush in his development as a top-class striker. He'd worked with Rushie and watched him in training; now he was playing alongside and learning even more from the master who was always talking to Robbie and encouraging him during games. It was the perfect combination and, of course, when Rushie inevitably moved on, Robbie was the natural successor to the goal king of the Kop.

The new heir to the throne has always been a confident lad, a typical scouser with a wicked sense of humour. But there was one occasion during a return flight from a European game against Vladikavkaz that he went a little too far and, famously, incurred the wrath of Razor. We were in high spirits after a victory and enjoying a celebration drink on the plane home when Steve Harkness thought it would be a good idea to relieve himself in Robbie's shoes as our young striker slept amidst the mayhem. When Robbie woke up, by which time I was fast asleep, he put his feet back in his shoes and quickly realised what had happened. Understandably, he wasn't too pleased and when he demanded to know who'd done it, the lads pointed to me. As a result, he went into my bag and pulled out my new pair of £300 Gucci boots and proceeded to cut them up, thinking he'd got his revenge on the dirty culprit who'd pissed in his shoes. Bad move. When I woke up as we came in to land, the lads were still in hysterics and it didn't take a genius to work out why. It wasn't until we were going through the airport that I confronted Robbie, told him that I'd had nothing to do with the original stunt and demanded that he bought me a new pair of boots to replace the ones he'd ruined. There was a big argument, a bit of pushing and shoving and having had enough of his bravado, I decided to teach him a lesson by punching him on the nose. Some of the other lads stepped in and although it was all over in a flash, the reporters who'd travelled with us were on the case and the story made the papers the next day.

Although the gaffer knew what had gone on, he didn't take action straightaway and it wasn't until a couple of days later that he called myself and Robbie in to read the riot act. But by then we'd already kissed and made up, and we've been the best of mates ever since. We laugh about it now.

The emergence of Robbie, as a striker rather than a prankster, was a major plus point in a season which promised so much at the start, but delivered so little as our challenge for a top three place fizzled out in the last couple of months after we'd looked as though we were adding some consistency to our game. We ended up finishing eighth, which was bitterly disappointing, but there was some consolation for me when Terry Venables, then the new national coach, called me into the England squad for a two-day training session at Bisham Abbey together with my Liverpool team-mates Rob Jones and Jamie Redknapp. There was no international coming up, but Terry wanted to have a look at a few players and I was delighted that he was aware of my progress since we parted company the previous summer. It transpired that he was also aware of the fact that I'd piled on a few pounds since the last time I saw him and he made a point of telling me that I could do with getting myself into better shape. I had put on a bit of weight, but I don't think it was affecting my fitness and it certainly wasn't affecting my performances for Liverpool. I'd had a couple of injuries that season and the fact that I'd been staying in a hotel for six months didn't do me any favours either because there's nothing much to do other than sitting around eating and drinking. Perhaps I had let myself go a little, but it wasn't a major problem and, as ever, it was the papers and not Terry or the Liverpool management who were making a big deal of it.

Having said that, there was a time that season when I hit the 15-stone mark and the club brought in a dietician who recommended sticking to things like Sugar Puffs, beans on toast and pasta and it seemed to do the trick. Ever since I was a teenager, I've had to watch my weight and I can't eat and drink what I want all the time, unlike a lot of people. Like a lot of players I enjoy a beer, when the time is right, but in the build-up to a game I have never touched anything, apart from the odd white wine and soda perhaps. Once the game is over though, I don't see anything wrong in letting your hair down. We were pretty good at that during those days. People might be alarmed if they knew the amount some players consume, especially at the current time with all the so-called alcohol-related problems of people like Paul Merson, Paul Gascoigne and Tony Adams, but you have to remember that we are naturally fit athletes who can handle it. We don't sit on our backsides all day and, if we have a few beers one night we will work it off in training the next day, eat and drink the right things and before you know it the alcohol is out of your system. It's not like we are doing it every day, just once in a while. I know the mentality has changed a little in this country with the influx of so many foreign players and the introduction of ultra-healthy continental methods, but there's still a time and a place for a good old booze-up. I still take my football as seriously as any of the foreign players or the teetotallers, but I've always been determined to enjoy my career to the full and I'd like to think I've done that and given the clubs I've played for pretty good service in the process. As so many other players have done in the past.

Nobody liked a drink more than Bryan Robson and look what he achieved in the game. The same applies to my old mate Jimmy Case down at The Dell. Now he could drink, and he taught me a thing or two I can tell you, but he was still playing at the age of 38 having won virtually all there is to win in the game, so it obviously didn't do him any harm. People at Liverpool still talk about the days when people like Casey and Terry McDermott used to drink others under the table and then play teams off the park.

Obviously the game was different in those days, the pace of the game was that much slower and fitness wasn't such a big issue. The other thing to remember is that the Liverpool team they played in was the best in Europe and, when you're successful you can get away with anything in the eyes of the fans. If we had a good win on a Saturday and went out for a few drinks in town, the supporters would love it and there would never be a shortage of people queuing up to buy you a beer. When you lose, it's a different matter though. Then you avoid the crowds and go for a quiet meal with the missus or something like that, because if fans see you out drinking and looking as though you are enjoying yourself after a defeat, that is something they can't accept. You would get loads of stick and they would use that against you time and time again if the team kept losing. It just wouldn't be worth the hassle. It's all about being sensible and knowing where, when and how much to drink. You get the odd person criticising you but they tend to forget that, while we are professional footballers and we get well paid for doing what we do, we are also human beings who like to do the things that normal people do from time to time.

CHAPTER NINE

Trouble with Refs and Reds

I t doesn't take a genius to work out that referees, and some linesmen, are not my favourite breed of human being on this earth. Some of them are simply too full of their own self-importance and tend to forget that the game is about the players and not them. Those officials who treat players with respect get it back in return but, sadly, there are very few of those about these days.

There was a time when you could enjoy a bit of banter with the ref and I have known a few down the years who have been perfectly capable of dishing out the verbals, and generally having a laugh with the players. That's the way it should be. But you can't say anything to officials now. If you do, you're never quite sure which way they are going to take it, so you end up saying nothing at all. Not to their face, anyway. Which is all very sad, because a friendly run-in with the ref used to be part and parcel of the game. At least it was when people like Roger

Milford, my favourite ref, was in charge. His white hair was always perfect, his tan was always topped up and he always had a smile on his face. You knew where you stood with him. You didn't take liberties and you respected him because he knew his stuff, but you could tell him what you thought of his decisions and he would just tell you what he thought of you. Now, though, you can't question a decision or ask an official to explain it because you end up with a caution and, ultimately, a ban – as I know only too well, having sat out a few games for arguing the toss with refs down the years. I'm no different to most players when it comes to backchat; you say things in the heat of the moment and it's normally borne out of frustration more than anything else.

I was a little surprised a few years ago when Keith Hackett, another referee I had previously had a lot of time for, decided to shoot his mouth off in the papers about players he didn't like. And even though I always thought I'd had a good relationship with him before he retired, my name was up there in lights alongside my former Manchester United rivals Bryan Robson and Paul Ince under the headline 'THE GOBFATHERS'. Hackett had a right go at us, saying that we were basically a pain in the arse and that we always questioned his decisions and always wanted to have the last word. Now I can understand him saying that about Incey(!), but not me. I can't say I was hurt by his comments though – in fact it was nice to be put in the same bracket as Ince and Robson – and I just put it down to the fact that poor old Keith must have been a bit hard up and needed the cash, so he sold his soul to the newspapers. I think he probably remembered an incident in one of his last games, at Old Trafford, when he originally awarded us a penalty but then spotted the linesman's flag and changed his decision. He ended up giving them a free-kick and, on that occasion, I did let fly with a few choice words and basically let him know that I thought he'd bottled it.

Sometimes I don't think referees appreciate the frustration you experience when a decision goes against you, especially in a big game, and that a lot of things are said in the heat of the moment. There's a lot of pressure on players at the highest level these days and I think more officials should try and understand that. They should also realise that players like me are passionate about the game and, as much as you attempt to curb your temper, there are going to be moments when you get a bit carried away.

As I've said before, once you get a reputation it's difficult to shake it off and referees seem to react differently when they're dealing with Neil Ruddock, Bryan Robson, Paul Ince and the like. But my disciplinary record has not been as bad as some people like to make out. I've been sent off five times in my career, only once during my spell at Liverpool, and I don't think that's too outrageous considering the fact that I'm a committed defender. Two of those were for professional fouls, so I think I've been unfairly branded. My old Southampton team-mate Francis Benali, a mild-mannered fella who didn't drink or swear but turned into a right little nutter once on the pitch, got sent more times than me, yet he has never been subjected to half the stick I've received. The strange thing is that, before a game, I will always have a laugh and joke with the ref – pinch his nuts, or something like that – and I tend to have a good rapport with most of them. But once the game starts their attitude towards me seems to change, the banter stops and suddenly I'm a marked man again. Just something I've had to learn to live with, I'm afraid.

I didn't miss many games through suspension during the early days at Liverpool and in my second season at Anfield, 1994–95, I was an ever-present apart from sitting out the last few games with an injury. We'd begun that season really well under Roy Evans, beating Crystal Palace 6–1 away, Arsenal at home and then my old club Southampton at The Dell. We only conceded five goals in the first seven league games and I capped a good start to the season, personally, by having the distinction of scoring the first goal in front of the newly re-opened Kop after the famous terracing had been replaced by seats. I scored in a 3–2 win over Aston Villa and things were set up nicely for a decent title challenge but, even though we only dropped out of the top five once, the Championship was just out of reach and we ended up finishing fourth. But the season was still a memorable one because it marked my first winners' medal – and my first (and only, as it turned out) international cap. I'd been called up for an England get-together the previous season but this was for real and it goes without saying that I was very, very proud and excited, although not entirely surprised as my name had been bandied about the papers for a while and, in my own mind, I knew I was playing well enough to be in with a chance. Terry Venables was aware that I'd been working hard at all aspects of my game, including my discipline and my fitness, and I was honoured that the man who had made me captain of Spurs was now giving me the chance to prove myself at international level.

But while my call-up to the England squad for the match against the United States had been predicted by some, the way the news was broken to me did carry a large element of surprise. I was spending the day at York races with the Liverpool lads when, suddenly, there was an announcement over the tannoy for me to go to the main office as there was an urgent message for me. All sorts of things were going through my mind – has there been an accident at home, are the lads having a wind-up? – but it transpired that Terry had phoned the course and left a message saying I had been called up to the England squad and needed to report for training at Bisham Abbey first thing in the morning. It was a fantastic feeling but the first thing that occurred to me was that, as I'd been on the beer all day and was well oiled by now, I'd better sober myself up pretty damn smartish. I went home to get a good night's sleep and left early next morning, armed with a packet of extra strong mints to hide the smell of the booze, to join up with Tel and the England boys. I made the bench against the USA and, although I didn't get on, I didn't feel deflated or disappointed; I was just pleased to be involved with the squad. It was great to work with Tel again and get a feel of the international set-up, having played at all other levels for my country. The atmosphere in the England squad was so relaxed, so friendly, and, while much of that was due to Terry's ability to bring players together, it was also down to the fact that the national team was playing only friendlies at that time, having qualified for Euro 96 as hosts. There wasn't much pressure in the build-up to games, or during them, and I think that helped me to settle in. I was delighted when, having had a taste of the international scene, I was called up for the next couple of squads for matches against Colombia and Romania – although once again the bench was as close as I got to winning my first cap. But I was beginning to feel more and more a part of the squad, which Terry helped gel even more by arranging get-togethers at Bisham Abbey from time to time. Euro 96 was only 18 months away and that was what the manager was working towards; and so was I.

Not that I was getting carried away with the fact that I'd been involved in squads for a few friendly internationals, but you have to set yourself targets and that was mine. Just as it was any player in or around the squad at the time.

The fact that the European Championships were being held in this country – the biggest football showpiece England has staged since the 1966 World Cup – was a fantastic incentive for all of us and the competition for places was fierce, and would become even more intense in the months ahead. For now though, I was quite content to be rubbing shoulders with the Gazzas, Shearers, Platts and Wrights of this world, having been accustomed to playing against them, not with them, Shearer aside. It did seem strange meeting up with the squad for the first time as a 'new boy', a bit like your first day at a new school, but the established players soon made me feel at home. I was still in awe of certain players though, notably Gazza who has such a massive presence – you definitely know when he walks into the room, put it that way! Even though he was recovering from injury at the time, Terry made a point of inviting him over from Lazio to be part of the squad and he was brilliant for morale. Everyone loved him.

I'd heard all the stories about him doing crazy things and getting involved in all sorts of stunts, but it's only when you're in his company for any length of time that you realise how mad he is; in the nicest possible way, of course. Little wonder Bobby Robson labelled him 'daft as a brush'. He's just one funny guy and you were never quite sure what he was going to do next.

During England get-togethers, we would all go to the cinema after training to pass the time away and that was usually the cue for Gazza to entertain the 100-strong crowd which he invariably attracted when he was out in public. One afternoon, we all turned up at the cinema half an hour early and weren't allowed into the auditorium because there was a guy in there still cleaning up from the previous showing. So we waited around for about ten minutes until the place was spick and span before taking our seats. It was then that Gazza came in with the biggest bucket of popcorn you have ever seen and as he went past me he made out I had tripped him up. As he went crashing to the floor (injured, remember!) the popcorn went flying everywhere. You should have seen the poor cleaner's face as we fell about in hysterics. Needless to say, Gazza pointed the finger of blame at me and I had to take the rap. Silly, childish some might say, but bloody funny. Having Gazza around the place, crocked or otherwise, was great for bringing the squad together and it certainly helped the new boys like me feel part of things.

Knowing Terry Venables and the way he works also helped the settling in process. I learned a lot from him during our brief time together at Spurs and even though we were only working together for a few days at a time with England, I was picking up new tips and pieces of advice from the best one-to-one coach I've known. He knows every position on the park inside out and he would pick up on things you weren't even aware of. Everyone had so much respect for him, not just for his coaching ability, but his supreme ability to make players feel comfortable in his company when the work was done. He would have a laugh and a joke with the players but, on the training field, he was deadly serious about his work. You listen and you act; otherwise you're out. A simple philosophy which worked. When I first joined up with the England squad he made a point of talking at some length to me, as he did with most of the boys, about what he expected of me and what I could add to the squad. 'I just want you to do what you've been doing for Liverpool and what I taught you at Spurs,' I remember him saying. He urged me not to change my game and not to do things differently just because I was now with the England squad. 'Do what you do best and that will be good enough for me.' That advice alone did me the world of good because, essentially, he was telling me not to try too hard to impress, but just be myself. He's the master at relaxing players and getting the best out of them.

After a few training sessions I felt I'd known the other players in the squad for years, not weeks or months. I even became firm friends with someone I'd only ever viewed before as an enemy, Ian Wright – who later became a West Ham team-mate of course. We were always at each other's throats during league games, especially when it was Arsenal v Spurs, and I've lost count of the number of run-ins we've had. Our rivalry went back to the days when Wrighty was at Crystal Palace and he partnered Mark Bright up front. Now those two were a real handful. Kick one and you were guaranteed a row with both of them; that's how close they were. Double-trouble. I can't remember any specific encounters but, basically, we didn't get on. There would always be a big build-up in the media who would bill it as 'RUDDOCK V WRIGHT' and, invariably, we didn't let them down. And it was never a case of forgetting about our differences once the game was over and sharing a laugh and a drink in the players' lounge, because we never spoke – apart from on the pitch, and then it was only to argue. He went his way and I went mine. We were the worst of enemies but became the best of friends when we were brought together in the England squad because we were fighting a common cause instead of each other. We were both lively, fiery characters and before we met up with England we only ever saw the horrible side in each other. But once we made the effort to get to know each other off the field, we got on like a house on fire. I can recall coming back from my first England get-together and my wife Sarah asking me which player I'd struck up the best rapport with and I said: 'You're not going to believe this, but I've become good pals with Wrighty.' Sarah was totally taken aback ('Not Ian Wright, no!') but, even though she never liked him because of all the stuff that had gone on between us, she too became great friends with Ian and his wife and we've remained close ever since. Once you get to know him, you can't help but like him and be affected by his incredible enthusiasm and passion for the game. He loved playing for his country – it meant everything to him – and I remember thinking 'That's the attitude I'm going to have when I pull on an England shirt'.

As it turned out, it wasn't too long before I did realise a lifelong ambition by winning my first cap in another friendly against Nigeria on 16 November 1994. With regular centre-halves Tony Adams and Gary Pallister, two great players I looked up to, ruled out because of injury, it wasn't a massive surprise when I was told by Terry's number two, Don Howe, three days before the game that I would be starting alongside Steve Howey in a new-look defensive partnership. But it was still a massive thrill and I couldn't wait to ring round everyone and tell them the good news. I was on the phone for ages, telling the whole world and his dog that I was about to become Neil Ruddock of Liverpool and England. Sarah was in tears, Mum cried her eyes out and even my dad and my two brothers had lumps in their throats and could hardly speak. I must admit I was pretty emotional too. It was what I had always dreamed of and it was only really when I'd started breaking the news to family and friends that the enormity of it all started to sink in.

Stepping into Tony Adams' shoes was quite a test because he'd developed into something of an England legend after taking a lot of stick earlier in his international career. I knew Tony socially because he used to drink in my local pub in Romford, The Chequers, and although it was common knowledge that he liked a pint, as they say, it never occurred to me that he had a serious problem with alcohol. He enjoyed a beer like the rest of us, but he always seemed as fit as a fiddle, his performances on the field didn't seem to be affected, so it was a big shock when he later came out and admitted to being an alcoholic. I've always looked upon him as a magnificent professional who, like Wrighty, loved and appreciated everything about being an England international footballer.

Suddenly, it was my turn to experience the pride of representing my country in a full international and because both Steve and I knew on the Monday that we were definitely starting the game, we had a few sessions to prepare and get used to playing alongside each other. That helped a lot and I'm glad I knew well in advance that I was playing rather than the manager revealing on the day of the game that I was going to make my debut. I'd probably have been a bundle of nerves if that had been the case; some say I was anyway. Once again, Tel got it spot on and he made sure we were nice and relaxed going into the match against a highly-fancied and very talented Nigerian side. Terry's great in the build-up to a game because not only will he tell you how to do your job properly, he'll make you aware of what your opponent is likely to do and how to combat that. He thinks of everything and looks at the game from all angles. Until I teamed up with him at Tottenham, I'd never really been coached like that; it opened my eyes to a whole new way of approaching the game. He makes you visualise certain things in your mind and think about how to deal with all sorts of situations. If you've got a good idea what your opponent is thinking, what he's likely to do next, already you are better equipped to handle him – and that's just one of the many things I've learned from Tel. It goes without saying, too, that he's a great motivator and even though the Nigeria game was seen by some as 'just another friendly' en route to Euro 96, he left you in no doubt it was much more than that. It certainly was for me; my England debut. My proudest moment. And I almost marked my debut in the 1–0 win with a goal. In fact, I would probably have been the goal hero of the night if David Platt hadn't nipped in front of me to score with a near post header. As the ball came into the box, courtesy of a Dennis Wise free-kick on the right, I remember thinking, 'this is mine' but at the time Platty was the ace goal poacher for England and he claimed the glory from me. Not that I was too bothered; I was just delighted to have had the experience of walking up the tunnel at Wembley wearing an England shirt with the three lions. A very proud moment. I can't remember much about the build-up or whether I was particularly nervous before the game but friends, especially my great mate Danny from Hornchurch, assured me I looked scared to death and as white as a sheet when I walked onto the pitch before the game. I'll have to take their word for it because everything went so quickly and I cannot recall too much about the game itself – apart from Platty stealing my thunder, that is.

I can't even remember the dignitaries whom we were introduced to before kick-off. It could have been the Queen Mum and I probably wouldn't have batted an eyelid. But one thing which sticks in my mind was spotting my mum and dad in the crowd as we walked towards the halfway line for the national anthem, and thinking how proud they must have been. All I could think about was playing well, following Terry's pre-match instructions and not letting anyone down. I was quite pleased with my performance, particularly in the second half, and I think Steve and I worked pretty well together once we'd settled down and got a nervy opening few minutes out of the way. Nigeria were no mugs and the likes of Efan Ekoku, Rashidi Yekini and Daniel Amokachi, who had only just played in the USA '94 World Cup finals, were quite a handful. I didn't get bad write-ups in the papers the next day so I was reasonably optimistic about staying in the squad, if not the starting XI, especially as Terry had been full of words of praise and encouragement. He told me to go away, carry on working hard at my fitness and generally gave me the impression I would be involved next time. England games were few and far between at that time because, as

Euro 96 hosts, we didn't have to qualify for the tournament which I was already setting my sights on. That wasn't being over-confident, or big headed; it was just that I'd had a taste of international football and was desperate for more. Everyone who was in or around the squad at that time really wanted to be part of such an historic occasion. I was no different. Sadly, things didn't work out that way for me because, by the time Terry named his next squad for a friendly later that season, I'd picked up an injury and, for whatever reason, I was never quite the same player again. I never regained the consistency I'd had during my year at Spurs and first two seasons at Liverpool, and the Nigeria cap was to prove to be my one and only.

I did captain England 'B' in a match against the Republic of Ireland when I was coming back from injury, but the full squad eluded me after that which was naturally a big disappointment to me. Of course, I would have loved to have gone on and won 50 caps for my country, but it wasn't meant to be and at least I can say I played for England. No-one can take that cap, that achievement, away from me. It's in the record books and I'm very proud of the fact that I've represented my country. There have been a lot of very good players before me, and there'll be a lot more after I've packed up, who never had that honour. I did, and I've got the cap, the shirt and the video to prove it. The fact that the game was at Wembley makes it extra special. If it had been on a meaningless tour of Australia, or away to the Faroe Islands or someone like that, it obviously wouldn't have meant so much. But I can say I've played for England at Wembley (and won!) and even though some people suggested at the time that I was 'one of Terry's boys' because we'd been together at Spurs and I'd backed him so strongly during his battle with Alan Sugar, I knew I had been picked on merit. I also know that I didn't look out of place against a useful Nigerian side either.

I think I showed a lot of people I could hold my own at that level and it's just a shame that a succession of injuries, together with a few personal problems, put paid to my international career.

Terry kept in touch with me and was keen to check on my injury situation from time to time. He did actually recall me to the squad at one point before Euro 96, but I had to decline the invitation because, both mentally and physically, I didn't feel right. I knew in my own mind I would not be able to do myself justice and there was no way I was going to join up with the squad and risk letting both myself and Terry down. As it transpired, the European Championships passed me by – which was a major disappointment – and that England cap against Nigeria remains my only one to date. I certainly never got a look-in after Terry left the national job and Glenn Hoddle took over, which is not surprising as injuries restricted my appearances for Liverpool for the next couple of years. But I've never given up hope of playing for my country again and even now I'm in my 30s I still harbour ambitions to pull on an England shirt. Stuart Pearce, now a West Ham team-mate, was given an international reprieve by Kevin Keegan at the age of 37, so perhaps there's still time yet to add to that solitary cap.

CHAPTER TEN

Scandal, Shame, and the End of the Anfield Road

The 1994–95 season was certainly proving to be an eventful one because, soon after I'd made my England debut, Liverpool were playing away at my old club Spurs and I had the misfortune to score an own goal past David James. It wasn't as if it was simply bad luck though. I should have put the ball in Row Z, but it slid under my studs and spun into the net. The last thing you want to do when you are playing against your former club is put the ball past your own keeper under any circumstances, especially as it gave Spurs a point they didn't deserve. For much of the game we absolutely battered them and should have added to Robbie Fowler's penalty, given all the possession we had enjoyed and chances we had created. I was gutted and all I could think about at the time was the smug look I knew there would be on Alan Sugar's face. To make matters worse, I later discovered that my 'old friend' had been mouthing off (again!) in the directors' box and was heard to say, with his usual sarcasm, something like 'Well done, Ruddock; I always knew he still wanted to play for Spurs'. No doubt Sugar thought he was being very funny in front of all his cronies, but he wasn't laughing a couple of days later when I told the papers that he was the one who still wanted me to play for Spurs, as he'd tried to sign me back no fewer than *five* times that season.

I think he tried to deny it, but my story was absolutely true. I was even told on one occasion that Ossie Ardiles, the Spurs boss, had been around to my house on his way back from a game at Manchester City to see me and ask if I fancied a move back to White Hart Lane. I wasn't at home at the time and Ossie called at the wrong house in any case. He went to a neighbour's house and they relayed the story to Liverpool chairman David Moores, whom they just happened to be related to. All very bizarre. But, even if I had been around at the time and spoken to Ossie, he couldn't have said anything to persuade me to give up Liverpool and return to Tottenham. Not unless he'd said Sugar was quitting. Even so, it was still very flattering that the club I'd left in such acrimonious circumstances wanted me back. Around that time, I was also getting loads of phone calls from different agents saying that Spurs were desperate to sign me, but I was happy at Liverpool and didn't want to leave. Why should I walk out on one of the biggest clubs in the world to go and work for a man I had no respect for? The calls I received were all from agents and I can't imagine that Alan Sugar would have had the balls to contact me direct. Basically it was a non-starter, purely and simply because of him. I couldn't even bring myself to talk to him again, let alone play for him.

There was also talk the same season that Glasgow Rangers had made a £4.5 million bid for me and that too was very flattering, but I was in no hurry to leave Liverpool and nothing came of that. Also, I had such a good relationship with everyone at Anfield, not least 'Mr Chairman', or 'Mooresy' as we sometimes called him on those less formal occasions – like the time I bumped into him on holiday in Marbella at the end of that season. Injuries and suspension meant I missed the last few games so the wife and I nipped off early and, ironically, the first people we met in Spain were the chairman and his family. He invited us to his hotel for a few drinks and when, at one point, I called him 'Mr Chairman' as normal, he turned round and said: 'You don't have to call me that when we're on holiday; call me Dave or Mooresy.' Can you imagine the Tottenham chairman saying to me 'Call me Al, or Shuggy'? I don't think so.

Mr Moores was a lovely man and I have to smile when I think of an incident one April Fool's Day when I was asked by Adidas, for whom I'd been testing their new Predator boots along with Jamie Redknapp and Paul Ince, to pose for a picture wearing 'The New Predator Headband'. The photo appeared in the paper together with a story about this amazing headband which would enable you to head the ball about 80 yards ... with swerve! When I bumped into the chairman the day the story appeared, he asked me in a worried voice: 'You're not *really* going to wear that headband, are you, Razor?' I had to point out that the date was 1 April and we had a good laugh about it.

155

While I was disappointed to miss the end of that 1994–95 season, I'd already had the consolation of picking up my first winners' medal of any note when we beat Bolton in the final of the Coca Cola Cup. I know it's not as grand and prestigious as the FA Cup and people like Alex Ferguson treat it as something of a 'mickey mouse' competition, but it's a Wembley occasion with a place in Europe at stake. We certainly took it seriously and we were worthy winners on a day which belonged to Steve McManaman, who was on fire and scored two magnificent goals in a 2–1 victory. We were coasting at one point but they pulled a goal back and, with only a minute to go, I gave away a stupid free-kick on the edge of the box and I can remember Jamie Redknapp looking at me and, even though he never said a word, I knew he was thinking 'You w*****, Razor'. It was a worrying moment because we were aware that Alan Thompson has a great left foot and was deadly in the sort of situation I had presented Bolton with. My overriding memory of the game was thinking at the time that, if they scored, it would all be my fault and I could have cost us the Cup. But, thankfully, 'Thommo' smashed his shot about 20 yards over the bar and there wasn't a more relieved man in the place than me. No sooner had we taken the goal kick than the final whistle went and it was time to party.

'Macca' won the Man of the Match award that day because of his two goals and all-round display, but we also owed our success to the brilliance of David James who produced one of the best saves I have ever seen in my life to deny Thompson in the first half. A lot of people criticised David during his time at Anfield, but I rate him as the greatest keeper I have played with and it's a shame he didn't get the recognition he deserved as a Liverpool player. I was delighted for him when he got a move to Aston Villa at the end of the 1998–99 season and I believe he will be a massive success there and prove a lot of people wrong. I just feel sorry for whoever has to room with him on away trips at Villa these days because David is prone to sleepwalking during the night, amongst other things, and has been known to scare the living daylights out of room-mates from time to time. As former Liverpool defender Torben Pieknik would testify. Now David is a lovely bloke, a bit of a gentle giant you might say, but he scared poor Torben to death once when he attacked him in the middle of the night. There was even a suggestion that David's wife had also been an unwitting victim of his night-stalking on one occasion, but maybe that was just a vicious rumour.

Anyway, back to the Coca Cola Cup final victory over Bolton. It was a great feeling to win a trophy at Wembley and it's just a shame we didn't go all the way in the FA Cup as well after reaching the sixth round. But Spurs, of all teams, beat us at Anfield and that was a massive disappointment. With the hamstring injury I picked up against Wimbledon at the end of May, a brilliant season ended on a sour note. Little did I know at the time that things were going to get even worse and that my best Liverpool days were behind me.

Despite enjoying an extended rest during the summer break, I was still struggling with the same injury at the start of the next season, 1995–96, and although I scored the winner against QPR in my comeback game at the end of August, my run in the team didn't last. After getting a recall to the England squad for a game against Colombia, and having half an eye on Euro 96, I was injured again after doing the splits and damaging my groin against Middlesbrough in November and that was basically the story of my season. I was out for about six weeks and while that meant I could *really* enjoy myself over the Christmas period, I would much rather have been playing regularly and putting myself back in the frame as far as England was concerned. It used to be a standing joke that, like Tony Adams, I was always injured or suspended over Christmas so I could let my hair down while the other lads were having to take it easy, lay off the booze and cram a load of games in. Strangely enough, it has been the case on a number of occasions but, this time, it was no laughing matter for me and I was beginning to get worried about the number of injuries I was picking up.

I made my next comeback against Leeds and scored twice in a brilliant 5–0 win, probably one of the best Liverpool performances I had been involved in, but then after two more games I was back on the treatment table, back on the sidelines and back in the doldrums. It was a constant battle to get fit and when I did regain fitness, I wasn't getting straight back in the team because other players had come in and done well in my absence.

When I did eventually regain my place and get a few games under my belt, I'd pick up another injury and it all became very frustrating. If I'd had another season like my first two at Liverpool, I'm sure I would have been a contender for the European Championship squad, but the longer the season wore, the further I fell down the pecking order. That was disappointing enough, but the biggest blow of all came right at the end of the season when I was left out of the FA Cup final side to face Manchester United, even though I'd played in the last four league games, plus the quarter-final and the semi-final, and was starting to feel like my old self again. I'd got it in my head that I was definitely, definitely going to play at Wembley.

Even up to the Thursday before the game Roy Evans had indicated he was going to stick with the same team that had started the last few games, but when we trained on the Friday afternoon, my birthday, I was running past Roy at one point and he said to me, 'I don't know how to tell you this, but…' And that was it, I was out of the final. What a birthday present, that was. I was so upset that I just told him to 'F*** off' and stormed off. I was in tears and couldn't believe I was being denied the chance to fulfil another childhood dream. I didn't even merit a place on the bench, for heaven's sake. I went off to have a few beers on my own, but trying to console myself was a hopeless task. I had never felt so gutted or let down. Every player wants to play in an FA Cup final and when it's Manchester United you are up against, it doesn't get any better than that.

If I'd thought my place was in doubt in the build-up to the game, I could probably have accepted it, but I was convinced I was playing up until two days before. So to be told on the eve of the game, on my birthday too, that I was being robbed of the chance to play in a Cup final at Wembley, I was distraught. I thought I had played well in the last few games but the manager decided to bring Phil Babb back into the team, alongside Mark Wright and John Scales, and that was me out. I might be a big bloke and have the reputation of being a hard man, but I cried like a baby when he dropped that bombshell. I had nothing against 'Babbsy', we were the best of mates, but it was the way the manager had handled the situation. If he'd told me earlier in the week, I could have understood it. At least then he would have had a few days to prepare his defensive strategy and it was amazing that he didn't settle on his team until the Friday. There was little or no time to prepare to play against one of the most potent strike forces in the country. Roy said he hated having to tell me that he was leaving me out, and he was quoted in the papers as saying that it was on a par with telling a 16-year-old apprentice that he isn't going to make it and that the club is letting him go. But no matter how sorry or how bad he felt about it, it didn't change the fact that I was going to miss the biggest game of my life. If anything, Roy's comments in the paper the next day made it worse. From that day on I lost a little respect for him and I'm sure the way I reacted caused him to lose a little respect for me too. But that's the way I am. I wear my heart on my sleeve and I tell people exactly the way it is.

It was the worst possible way to end the worst season of my career so far and I took no delight from the fact that the lads lost the game to an Eric Cantona goal. It was a bit of a sloppy goal to give away and the way we defended the situation made me think that I could perhaps have done something about it – closed him down, blocked his shot, anything – but the damage was done.

From then on my Liverpool career went even further downhill because, the following season, I had problems to contend with off the field as well as on. Whether the disappointment and frustrations of what had happened to me, professionally, over the previous 18 months caused me to go off the rails, I don't know. But that's what happened and I almost wrecked everything I'd worked for in a crazy, six-month spell during which I

ove: I had to give Robbie a slap after
e away trip, but I forgave him for trying
cheat on this occasion.

ght: Bruce looking dapper but a bit
vous on his way to court. I know how
feel, mate.

erever you go there are hangers-on and here are ten 'saddos' sucking up to pop legend
bie Williams on an end-of-season tour.

It's no wonder Kenny Dalglish is looking down in the mouth. I've just snubbed him and Blackburn to sign for Liverpool.

Kevin Keegan and Newcastle didn't even get a look-in once I'd spoken to Graeme Souness.

That's how I looked when 'that nice man' Roy Evans left me out of the Liverpool team for the 1996 FA Cup Final!

A Starr in the making! 'Ringo' Ruddock looks the part for a Liverpool photoshoot.

Gary Pallister gets close to Stan Collymore. Which is more than we ever did as team-mates.

I'd have stopped Cantona scoring the FA Cup winner in 1996 – if I'd been selected, that is!

Left: Who are you calling a Spice Boy? Perhaps a cream suit for the 1996 FA Cup Final wasn't such a bright idea after all.

Far Right: Signing for West Ham along with Javier Margas who did a runner because he didn't like the soft pitches, allegedly.

Right: Andy Cole keeps well away this time, which is not surprising considering that I broke both his legs once.

Glenn Hoddle is one of the finest footballers I have played alongsi but as for being England manage

West Ham boss Harry Redknapp makes his point in his usual cool, calm and calculated manner.

Another red card, this time against Leeds in December 1998. Ah well, another Christmas off!

Having fun with son Josh and daughter Millie at Lake Windermere during a rare break. Or was I suspended?

Right: Wife Sarah (right) and Alan Shearer's wife Lainya have become close friends since our Southampton days.

I've always told people that 'Razor Ruddock' is a thoroughbred. Well this one is. The horse isn't mine, sadly, but it's won me a few quid in its time.

could say
as quite
ased with
goal in the
bbing of
by in
8/99.

Above, top: Eyal Berkovic is just happy that the operation to return his head to its rightful place was a success. John Hartson's left foot is okay, too.

Above, middle: I play the role of referee Paul Alcock as Paolo Di Canio talks me through his controversial dismissal.

Patrick Vieira aims a mouthful of spit at me during the game with Arsenal at Upton Park in October 1999. I'm amazed how I managed to keep my cool under such provocation.

Young Joe Cole made a big impression during the early part of o 1999/2000 campaign before injury wrecked hi chances of taking part in Euro 200C

There were times during my inactive winter of 2000 when I wondered whether I'd be better off training huskies.

made Gazza look like a saint. In addition to the personal problems I was experiencing, I was injured for a lengthy period and that didn't help because the longer I spent on the sidelines, the more frustrated I became. Light training and treatment, followed by more light training and treatment, was pretty much the order of the day and I became increasingly depressed about the whole situation. Instead of thinking positively and saying to myself, 'I'm a professional footballer with one of the best clubs in Europe' and acting accordingly, irrespective of the problems I was having, I simply went off the rails. That's the only way I can describe it.

The summer of 1996, after the disappointment of the FA Cup final, was depressing to say the least and the fact that the European Championships were happening made things even worse. I couldn't help thinking what might have been. After all, it wasn't that long beforehand that I'd been in the England squad, was playing well for a great club and apparently on course to play in the finals of an international tournament. In this country too. I had desperately wanted to be a part of what promised to be a fantastic competition, especially with Terry Venables saying farewell at the end of it and with the whole country buzzing in anticipation. So, as you can imagine, I was pretty cheesed off throughout the summer but, after drowning my sorrows for the three weeks that Euro 96 was taking place, I decided I was going to do everything I possibly could to get my career at Liverpool back on track; prove the manager wrong by reacting positively to a negative situation. If anything, what had happened in the previous month or so strengthened my resolve and made me more determined than ever to re-establish myself in the team.

When I returned from holiday I worked really hard in pre-season and, after clear-the-air talks with Roy Evans, made a conscious effort to try and put the disappointments behind me. I was desperate to show him I still had plenty to offer Liverpool Football Club and, in return, he showed his commitment to me by offering me a new, five-year contract.

By this time my anger had cooled and we both realised there was no point in bearing grudges, or carrying on a personal feud which would have served little or no purpose for me, him or the club in general. When we had our heart-to-heart during the summer, he made a point of apologising for leaving me out of the Wembley squad and as good as admitted that he'd dropped a clanger by not playing me against United.

He said it had been his decision and that, in hindsight, it was probably the wrong one which was big of him to admit and went some way towards restoring my respect for him. We agreed to let bygones be bygones and he told me that if I reported back fit and raring to go, I would definitely be in his plans for the new season. That was reassuring to hear and I was more than happy to put pen to paper on a new, improved contract which would virtually have taken me to 33 and, as such, would probably have meant me spending the rest of my playing career at Anfield. That's what I wanted and, despite what had happened, it hadn't really entered my head to demand a move or rock the boat. What had gone on between me and Roy was history as far as both of us were concerned. He realised he had hurt me badly, and this was his way of showing his loyalty to me, which I appreciated. I think the chairman David Moores, whom I had always had a great relationship with, also had a say in the matter and it was good to know that I was still wanted and that we could all start the new season with a clean slate.

Even before we reported back for pre-season training, I was in good shape because I had been staying down in London and working out with the athletics' coach at Crystal Palace. I worked my nuts off on the running track and in the gym and even before I went back to Liverpool to start pre-season training for real, I was feeling really fit and supremely optimistic about the new campaign. However, about a week before the first game of the new Premiership season against Middlesbrough, who had just signed the Italian striker Fabrizio Ravanelli, I pulled my groin in training and was forced to miss the kick-off. After putting in so much effort to get myself into the best possible condition for the start of the season, this latest injury setback was soul-destroying. I'd damaged my groin the previous season, when I did the splits ironically also against Middlesbrough, and although this wasn't a recurrence of that problem it did give me a lot of cause for concern. Looking back, it was probably a result of me doing *too much* work during the summer and perhaps asking too much of my body, too soon. I hadn't given my muscles enough time to rest. I just couldn't believe my luck; I couldn't believe I was being made to pay the penalty for being too keen to prove my fitness to the manager – and to the fans who might have been questioning my attitude after the fall-out with Roy Evans. I was gutted.

It was another setback I could have done without, but it wasn't a disaster and the physios and doctors predicted that it would be weeks, not months, before I'd be back playing again, which was reassuring. Even so, it was frustrating to have to sit and watch the lads get off to one of the best starts Liverpool had enjoyed to a league campaign for years. Stan Collymore, having joined the club for a record £8.5 million from Nottingham Forest in 1995, was settling in and Patrik Berger, one of the Czech Republic stars at Euro 96, was an exciting addition to the squad. With Steve McManaman, Robbie Fowler and John Barnes also displaying their own particular talents at the start of the season, the prospect of a serious tilt at the Premiership title was a genuine one, especially when the lads blasted their way to the top of the table after winning six and drawing two of the opening eight games.

The goals were flying in – we scored 18 in those first eight Premiership matches – and, even more impressively, we'd only conceded three in the process. I didn't really make much of a contribution during the first few months, coming on as sub a couple of times as I battled to regain my match fitness following the injury, but when I did eventually start a game, I didn't take long to announce 'I'm back'. Within 13 minutes of my first full appearance, against Leeds at Elland Road, I was on the scoresheet and when Steve McManaman added a second in the closing stages, it wrapped up another impressive win. It was great to be involved again and I managed to keep my place for the next 12 league games, during which time we lost only once, at home to Sheffield Wednesday, to reclaim top spot over Christmas. December was a great month for us and there was such a tremendous feeling of pride and optimism around the place which had probably been lacking in recent seasons. The Anfield crowd was right behind us, the team was playing well as a unit, I was back on top of my game; and the results were going our way. Things couldn't have been better as we entered the New Year, 1997.

Everyone was on a high and I can remember at that time thinking back to something Graeme Souness had said to me at the time I was considering joining Liverpool from Spurs. Although I didn't really need much persuading to put pen to paper, I can recall Graeme telling me 'When things are going well and the team is top of the table, there isn't a better place in the world to play than Liverpool FC'. He was absolutely right. I also remember him countering that statement by warning me that it could also be a pretty miserable place to play when things were going badly. He was right on that score, too. At that time though, Anfield was Utopia and we really had the feeling that this could be our year. Mine, too.

I was pleased with my form and, although there had been no solid indication from Terry Venables' England successor Glenn Hoddle that I was in his thoughts, I was beginning to think that if I continued to perform consistently well, maybe an international recall wasn't out of the question, after all. Terry had called me up the previous season but the personal problems I had been experiencing, coupled with the niggling injuries, meant I had to turn him down. I hate to say it, but I wasn't interested in playing for my country at that time. It was different now, though. I was playing with such confidence that I believed anything was possible.

Sadly, and not for the first time in recent seasons, my hopes of an extended run in a successful team with its sights set on the title, were dashed when I picked up yet another injury in a goalless draw with West Ham in January. It was a similar problem to before, the groin, and meant another three months on the sidelines. My season was as good as over and I was resigned to twiddling my thumbs for a few weeks before starting my latest fight to recapture my fitness. It seemed to be a never-ending battle during that period and all the old frustrations began to creep back. We didn't really do much physical work at Liverpool, training sessions mainly revolved around games of five-a-side, so maybe the fact I wasn't working my body to its full extent during the week wasn't the ideal preparation for big games at the weekend. That's the only thing I can put it down to.

Until this last year, I had been fortunate with injuries, but all of a sudden I was picking up one after another. Nothing too serious, but enough to rule you out for a month or two and then you've got the problem of continually trying to recapture your match fitness and sharpness. Games at the highest level in this country are so physical and are played at such a tremendous pace these days that your body really needs to be in tip-top condition to survive the rigours of a whole season. Perhaps mine wasn't and maybe that was down to the training methods at Liverpool, which hadn't really changed since the halcyon days of the 1970s and 1980s. At that time, when the great Liverpool teams were picking up trophies every season, the club seemed to pride itself on the fact that training sessions were little more than a five-a-side kickabout. But the game was different then. The physical demands are so much greater now and perhaps the training methods favoured by Roy and the coaching staff had not improved along with the standard, and the power of play, in the Premiership.

Once again, I was feeling really low because after such

a promising spell the only goal I could set myself was getting back in time to play the last two or three games of the season. As it turned out, that's exactly what happened, but by the time I'd returned to the side we'd blown any chance we had of winning the title. More frustration. We'd been up there with the leading pack all season, but our championship challenge evaporated when we lost two home games on the trot, against Coventry and then Manchester United who went on to take the title.

Once again the problem of inconsistency reared its ugly head and we failed to make the most of a magnificent opportunity to put the club back up there alongside the likes of United and Arsenal as one of the dominant forces in English football. We ended up finishing fourth to claim a UEFA Cup place, which was not a bad achievement, but for Liverpool Football Club it was just not good enough. We didn't want to be remembered as also-rans or under-achievers; but we had to accept such accusations because, from being in a strong position in the league, we let our standards slip at crucial moments. The best sides, the successful sides, don't do that. It was a similar story of 'nearly, but not quite' in Europe, where we came back from 3–0 down in the away leg of the Cup-Winners' Cup semi-final to Paris St Germain and gave the French a scare by going 2–0 up in the second leg at Anfield. But our efforts were in vain because we couldn't get the all-important third goal to level the tie and we were out. Close, but no cigar, as they say.

Flopping in Europe (again!) was disappointing enough, but the most galling thing was seeing our bitter rivals from Manchester lifting the Premiership title once again and confirming the gulf which continued to exist between our two clubs. There's certainly no love lost between us and United, but even the most ardent Liverpool supporter had to accept that they were the best because they were the most consistent. We were never going to win the title unless we got that side of our game right. United had done us again, as they had done in the FA Cup final the previous year, and it hurt. Yet, as much as you have to admire Alex Ferguson's team for what they have achieved throughout the 1990s, you can understand why so many people hate them to a large degree.

But my personal dislike of the arrogance of certain individuals certainly had nothing to do with an incident which left United striker Andy Cole with two broken legs after a clash with yours truly. I would never deliberately set out to break an opponent's leg; not even a United player. Yet that was the accusation levelled at me after a full-blooded, yet fair, tackle on the former Newcastle striker (in a reserve game, no less) left him with fractures in both legs. Like myself, Andy was on his way back from injury and, even though this was a second team game, it was played with all the passion and commitment of a Premiership clash between two clubs who simply don't get on. It was never my intention to hurt him. I've got nothing against Andy Cole and enjoyed his company when we'd been on international duty for England or England 'B'.

The incident, at Anfield just a week or so before the senior sides met for real, was a 50–50 affair which I was determined to win, just as I am with every challenge I commit myself to make. There was no way I was just going to let him waltz past me en route to goal, even if it was only a reserve match. It was a whole-hearted attempt on my part to win the ball and I ended up landing on Andy and breaking both his legs, although I didn't know how bad his injuries were until I read the papers the next day. I wasn't even booked for the challenge, so my conscience was clear. Even so, I tried to make contact with him to see how he was and the people at Liverpool rang the hospital where he was being treated several times but without managing to get through. Whether he was prepared to speak to me or not, I don't know, but I was quite happy to say I was sorry to hear about the extent of the injuries and wish him all the best for a speedy recovery.

Strangely enough, although I was branded Public Enemy No.1 by some United fans who slaughtered me when I was on the bench for the Premiership game at Old Trafford a few days later, others actually stopped me in the street and thanked me. Andy was getting a bit of stick from a section of the Old Trafford crowd around that time and some of the more cynical supporters were quite happy about the fact he was going to be out of the first team firing line a bit longer. Cruel, or what? I knew, however, that I was going to get a hostile reception when Liverpool went to Old Trafford less than a week after the incident. But I was ready for them. I ran out for the warm-up with loads of cotton wool stuffed in my ears and made out I couldn't hear their boos and abuse, and wasn't bothered what they thought of me. I think that took the sting out of the situation a little and I enjoyed quite a comfortable afternoon.

It wasn't the first time I'd crossed swords with the United fans at Old Trafford and I doubt I will ever be forgiven for having the audacity to insult their former idol Eric Cantona by daring to turn down his infamous, turned-up collar during a league game the previous season. It was a pre-meditated thing and came out of a bet I'd had with a friend of mine from Liverpool, a local comedian called Willie Miller, who dared me to feel the great man's collar for a laugh. Not wishing to disappoint, I agreed to take up the challenge and as I was marking Cantona there were plenty of opportunities to carry out the dirty deed, which I did time after time, after time. I could tell he'd got the hump after I'd turned his collar down initially and by the fourth occasion he was so wound up that he swung an elbow at me and just missed my face. Undeterred, I did it again and again, and again until he snapped completely and launched into a knee-high tackle on me from behind, for which he got a yellow card. It was a bad challenge and the sort you would automatically receive a red card for these days, but I was glad he stayed on because it gave me another opportunity to wind him up again. Although I was in a bit of pain from his challenge, I wasn't going to let him know that he'd hurt me, so I got straight up and carried on with the game. When I re-adjusted his collar for the umpteenth time he turned round, looked me straight in the face with these mad, bulging eyes and yelled: 'Me and you, we fight in ze tunnel.' He had the look of a lunatic and I knew I'd pushed him too far; he was fuming. There was still a few minutes left and I remember thinking, 'It's all going to kick off here', so I prepared myself for a confrontation with the fiery Frenchman. When the final whistle went at the end of an exciting 2–2 draw, he dashed for the tunnel and so, assuming that he would be waiting for me, I went over to our keeper David James – the biggest bloke in our team – and told him to walk off with me. Brave, or what? As it turned out, Cantona wasn't waiting in the tunnel and the Anglo-French war was off. For now. Next stop, the players' lounge.

One great thing about the Liverpool lads was that, whatever the result, we would always go for a drink with the opposition afterwards, and it became something of a post-match ritual that we would always beat them to the bar. We had a saying 'Win, draw or lose; first to the bar for booze' and we invariably were. That was certainly the case on this occasion and I was happily enjoying a pint with the lads when I felt a tap on my shoulder and turned round to find Monsieur Cantona standing right behind me. My first thought was that he wanted to continue where we'd left off on the field but, instead, he produced a pint of lager and as he handed it to me he gave me a little wink and walked off. End of story.

CHAPTER ELEVEN

Mersey Misery, East End Delight

If the 1996–97 season had been a disappointment, the following year – my last at Anfield, as things turned out – was a disaster. I'd managed to get a few games under my belt after recovering from the latest injury setback and spent the summer of '97 working hard to make sure I was in tip-top nick for the start of the 1997–98 campaign. Pre-season went really well and I was looking forward to helping the club build on what we'd achieved the previous year.

Okay, we hadn't won anything and it was frustrating for all concerned that we'd allowed our Championship challenge to fizzle out, but there was still a feeling of optimism around the place. We'd made a couple of useful signings in the shape of German international Karlheinz Riedle, and Oyvind Leonhardsen from Wimbledon and, with the emergence of a certain Michael Owen, hopes were high that we could get it right this time.

The fact Roy Evans had managed to offload Stan Collymore was also seen as a positive move because, quite frankly, he was more trouble than he was worth and simply didn't fit in at Anfield. When the club had originally signed Stan from Nottingham Forest, at the start of the 1995–96 season, I thought he would prove to be a great signing but it just never worked out – and Stan must take a large portion of the blame for that. We knew he had a reputation as a bit of a loner, but he just made no effort to mix with the lads and be part of 'the team'. On his day he was brilliant, as a striker he'd got the lot, but you just never knew when he was going to deliver the goods. When he started off he really looked the part and I honestly thought he and Robbie Fowler would make the perfect combination up front. But he only seemed to turn it on when he felt like it, and he didn't exactly endear himself to his team-mates when he was quoted in a magazine article as saying that he was disappointed with the service he was getting and that, when he joined Liverpool, he expected to be surrounded by better players. He was going through a bit of a bad time, the goals weren't flowing as he'd hoped and promised, and so he turned on the other players in the team when he should have been looking at himself. He also said that we should adapt to his style and not the other way round. Hardly the brightest thing to say when you've just joined a new club. When the lads read what he'd said, the attitude of virtually everyone in the squad was 'F**k you, Stan'. Any respect we might have had was gone. If he'd actually confronted us and said 'Look lads, I was misquoted' or denied that he'd said those things, we could have forgiven him. But he didn't try to hide the fact, so as far as we were concerned he'd slagged us off to the media and you can't tolerate something like that. He did have clear-the-air talks with Roy Evans from time to time, but even then he would always have his agent Paul Stretford with him. He never had the balls to deal with the problem himself. And it was a problem, no doubt about it. Stan didn't make any attempt to get on with the lads and, although I used to sit next to him on the coach and try and make conversation with him, I could never claim to know him. Nobody did. He'd turn up for training, do his work, get changed and go home. Not exactly conducive to good team spirit, so I think most of the lads were relieved when he was finally flogged off to Aston Villa. Liverpool has always been a sociable club and he just didn't fit in.

Even when things weren't going so well on the field, the lads would stick together and apart from the last year or so when injuries took their toll, I will always look back on my time at Anfield with great fondness. I met some fantastic people, made some great friends and had a lot of laughs; many of them at the expense of dear old Jason McAteer who was naïve (some say, stupid) to the extreme. He was a gem, a real one-off whom we all loved to bits. Some of the daft things he did will go down in Anfield legend, like the time when he was filling in an application form for a credit card and had me in stitches when he got to the question about 'position held in company'. I was quietly reading my paper on an away trip when he suddenly piped up: 'What shall I put here, Razor, right-back or midfield?' Priceless. Even better was the occasion when he locked his car keys inside his car and a policeman stopped and offered assistance. The copper told him to go inside his house and get a coat hanger, so Jason reappear-ed a few minutes later with a wooden hanger! Phil Babb was with him at the time and couldn't believe his eyes. Different class. There was also an occasion, on a return flight from a European match, when we got into an argument over a game of cards and he suddenly jumped up and offered to take me on outside … at 30,000 feet!

Jason was subsequently nicknamed 'Dave' by way of a tribute to the great *Only Fools and Horses* character 'Trigger', which just happened to be the nickname of another Anfield star renowned for being a little slow on the up-take. Rob Jones, not the brightest bloke in the world, bless him, was often a figure of fun for choice comments like the one he made about a mate's forthcoming wedding. Rob explained to the lads that he had never met the bride, and asked in all innocence: 'How will I recognise her?' It wasn't until we pointed out that she might just be the one wearing a bloody great white dress and a veil that his mind was put at rest. And I'm sure it was Rob who responded over lunch to Ian Rush's request to 'pass the ketchup' by asking: 'What colour, red or brown?' Sadly, Rob's unintentional one-liners are no longer heard in and around the dressing room these days as he has been forced to retire because of a recurring knee injury. After failing to reclaim a place in the Liverpool side, he joined my current club West Ham on loan but, after desperately trying to recover his fitness, he was forced to call it a day. What happened to him is a dreadful shame, because he was once rightly hailed as the best full-back in the country when he first burst onto the scene with Liverpool and England. A lot of people said at the time that he would be England's first choice right-back for the next ten years and, but for a cruel spate of injuries and operations, I'm sure they would have been proved right.

Dominic Matteo was another young Liverpool player not exactly blessed with the greatest speed of thought. We had been out together for a couple of drinks one night and decided to pick up a takeaway pizza on the way home. He asked me what I was ordering and when he agreed to have the same I asked him if he wanted it cut into 16 pieces or eight. It was at that point 'Hombre', as we called him, replied: 'Better make it eight; I don't think I could manage to eat 16!'

Even the gaffer, Roy Evans, was prone to dropping the odd verbal clanger and giving the lads plenty of ammunition for a spot of micky-taking. One 'foot-in-mouth' classic came during a training session when he suddenly blurted out: 'Okay, we'll play us seven versus you seven, in a 20-minute, five-a-side match for half an hour!' Work that one out if you can. And he was supposed to be our leader! Only joking, Roy. Whilst I'm in full mickey-taking mode, I can't let my good mate Jamie Redknapp escape without a mention. One day after training I asked 'James' if he was coming out for a drink with the lads that evening and instead of coming out with the customary 'Do bears s**t in the woods?' response to such a ridiculous question, or 'Has Judith Chalmers got a passport?' he quipped in all seriousness: 'Is the Pope a Jew? Of course I'm coming out.' Like I said from the outset, never a dull moment.

Most of the lads liked a flutter on the horses and a day at the races was a popular pastime for people like myself, Robbie Fowler and Steve McManaman. One visit to Cheltenham did land us in trouble after the press concocted a story that we'd got drunk and smashed up the hospitality box we'd taken over for the day. We were good friends with the former champion jockey Tony McCoy and were invited down to Cheltenham to cheer him on. Tony won a hat-trick of races that day and, because we'd backed him all the way, all the lads were several thousands of pounds to the good. We were in high spirits, there's no doubt about that, but the next day the story in the papers was that we'd caused havoc at the race track and had wrecked the box, all of which was totally false. The papers also suggested that Paul Ince had been involved in a fight, but once again that was absolute nonsense as was borne out by the fact that we sued the paper concerned and came away with a few more quid as a result. But that was typical of the sort of thing which was going on at the time and it seemed that, wherever we went as Liverpool players, we were always up to no good and causing trouble. We couldn't seem to do anything without stories being invented in the press, no doubt by jealous people who didn't like the idea of us going out and enjoying ourselves when we weren't preparing for games. Or maybe they were just resentful of the fact that we were getting so well paid 'just for playing football'. There were so many lies being written about us at the time that it became something of a standing joke.

Going back to the start of my final season at Liverpool, that was anything but a laughing matter. Having got myself fit during the summer, again, I twisted my knee in the long grass at Wimbledon on the opening day of the season and suddenly I was back on the sidelines. I returned to the side for the Merseyside derby clash in October, a game we lost 2–0 at Goodison, and that proved to be my final appearance in a Liverpool shirt. I continued to work hard in training and was prepared to bide my time until someone got injured or their form dipped, but I never got further than the subs' bench and it was during this frustrating spell that I began to wonder if I had a future at Anfield. The writing was on the wall when Roy Evans called me in one day and asked me how I felt about going on loan, to somewhere like Bradford or Portsmouth, and I knew then my days were numbered. I still felt I had a lot to offer Liverpool but clearly the gaffer had other ideas, so I thought I'd test the water by asking him if I could move outright at the end of the season if I could find a club. Typically, he couldn't or wouldn't give me an answer there and then and he told me he would put my request 'to the board' as he would always do when confronted with contentious issues. In other words, he had to seek the permission of chief executive Peter Robinson who effectively ran the club and was responsible for making key decisions, not the manager. I never really had a bust-up as such with Roy, although I let him know I was disappointed with the way the situation was being handled and that I thought I deserved better treatment.

Basically they wanted me out, off the payroll, and that saddened me, even though I'd had a lot of injury problems which must have influenced their decision. I say 'their' decision because I don't believe for a minute that it was Roy's and Roy's alone. He didn't have that much control. Mr Robinson was the main man and he let you know it. He could be arrogant at times and if you saw him around the club, some days he would talk to you and other days he would blank you completely. You never knew where you stood with him and, as far as he was concerned, the players were simply employees of the football club he ran and that was it. He was in control and if he said that he wanted to ship players out because of the wage bill, then that's what Roy had to do. I just happened to be one of those players.

Mr Robinson may have been pulling the strings but, as far as my future was concerned, the ball was very much in my court because I still had three years of my contract to run. I could have played out my time in the reserves at Anfield, gone through the motions and picked up my money every month, but that's not the way I am. I wanted first team football, which is why I eventually decided to go on loan to Queens Park Rangers for whom I played the final seven games of the season (incredibly, we drew them all!) and helped them avoid the drop into Division Two by a point. I didn't really fancy it at first and thought I would hang around at Liverpool until I could get a permanent move sorted out. But after speaking to manager Ray Harford, whom I knew through Alan Shearer when they worked together at Blackburn, I decided to join them until the end of the season. At least I was playing meaningful football, proving my fitness and putting myself in the shop window. There was no going back to Liverpool now and, having returned to London, that was where I wanted to stay. I had always planned to go back to the capital at some stage of my career, so now was as good a time as any. That's not to say that I wouldn't have been prepared to see out my contract at Liverpool if I'd still been playing first team football, but that wasn't the case and it was pretty clear I'd reached the end of the line at Anfield. I had no hard feelings towards Roy and, apart from our occasional differences of opinion, I'd like to think we parted on good terms and he appreciated the service I'd given to Liverpool. I even sent him and Sammy Lee a 'thank you' card for all they had done for me and, during the summer, we all met up for a few drinks at Paul Ince's party and I'm glad to still class them both as friends. If anything, I felt a little sorry for Roy because I don't think he actually enjoyed the man-to-man management side of the job which he found difficult. I wouldn't say the players at Liverpool took advantage of him because he was such a nice, mild-mannered guy, but he didn't like confrontation and, perhaps, that was ultimately his downfall. Maybe there were times when he wasn't forceful enough, but ranting, raving and bawling people out wasn't his style and I think he was respected by the players for that.

Apart from denying me an FA Cup final appearance, I don't hold anything against him, although that will go down as the biggest disappointment of my Liverpool career. Other than that I have no regrets about my time at Anfield, I just wish I hadn't suffered as many injuries as I did at a crucial time in my career. If I hadn't spent so much time on the treatment table and had been playing regular first team football throughout, I wouldn't have gone off the rails the way I did. But that's in the past and I can't change what happened, even though, from time to time I think what might have been – certainly in terms of international recognition – if circumstances had been different. It's all ifs, buts and maybes and there's no point in dwelling on what might have been. The important thing once I'd made the decision to leave Liverpool was finding a new club where I would be happy and still have a chance of achieving success before hanging up my boots. West Ham turned out to be that club.

I'd spoken to manager Harry Redknapp earlier in the

season, which I was perfectly at liberty to do as Liverpool had told me I could find another club, and when the opportunity arose to join them in the summer it was too good to turn down. I knew Harry socially through Jamie, not just from our Liverpool days together but when he was a young lad at Bournemouth before we'd both made our mark in the game. There had been talk about West Ham being interested in me before I'd actually signed my last five-year contract at Liverpool but, at the time, I wanted to stay at Anfield and nothing materialised. But we kept in touch and when things began to turn sour on Merseyside, Harry told me to give him a call if I wanted to get away, and that's exactly what I did. I actually phoned him, after my agent had spoken to him, and basically asked him to take me on. He wasn't in a position to sign me once the transfer deadline had passed, hence my decision to go on loan to QPR, but once the season was over all parties were able to reach an agreement in time for the start of the new campaign. Nottingham Forest showed an interest in me and I think QPR would have liked to have taken me on permanently if they could have come up with the cash, but once I knew Harry was seriously interested I'd set my heart on going to Upton Park.

I'd always had a lot of respect for Harry, both as a person and a manager, and a lot of people had told me what a great bloke he was to work for and I was delighted to sign for him in time for the start of the 1998–99 season. It was also a case of joining a friendly, family club which had long had a reputation for looking after their players and, obviously, that entered into the equation. Plus, the club had been making great strides under Harry and was then in a position to challenge for honours, perhaps not the Premiership title, but the domestic cups and, of course, a place in Europe. You could say that, in terms of size and stature, West Ham were not as big as Liverpool but the club was moving in the right direction and there was a better opportunity for me to be playing first team football on a regular basis, which was the most important thing.

I knew I couldn't expect to walk straight into the team, however, and that I would have to prove myself along with all the other members of what was a gifted squad made up of experienced players like Ian Wright and Steve Potts, along with talented, homegrown stars like Frank Lampard and Rio Ferdinand. So I didn't view it as a step down; I saw it as a great challenge and the chance to prove I could still perform at the highest level.

I know people had been questioning my fitness after the injury problems I'd had in my last couple of years at Anfield, but I was confident I'd got a good few years left in me as a Premiership player and it was heartening for a manager of Harry's stature to show faith in me. Before I signed he did question me about my fitness and whether my weight was stable, and I assured him that despite the fact I hadn't played much top flight football in the previous year or so, I was still in good shape and that I could do a good job for him. He went on record at the time I joined, on the same day as West Ham signed the Chilean Javier Margas, as saying that a fit Neil Ruddock would be a great addition to the squad and I'd like to think I've lived up to his expectations and justified the faith he showed in me at a time when Liverpool didn't think I had anything left to offer them. I sailed through my fitness test and signed a three-year deal, so everything was set up for an exciting season at a club renowned for its passionate supporters who, thankfully, seemed to take to me straightaway. My wife Sarah is an East London gal, born not a million miles away from Upton Park, so maybe that helped!

The place was buzzing as the first game of the season, away at Sheffield Wednesday, approached and Harry reckoned that was due in no small part to the effect Wrighty, an amazing and bubbly character as we all know, and myself had had on the other players at the club. Apparently, before we arrived the dressing room was a bit quiet and needed an injection of life. I'd like to think Wrighty and myself provided that, certainly Ian. Players seemed a little reserved and almost embarrassed to let their hair down, let their emotions show in the dressing room before a game when nerves are at their peak. I've always believed that you should let that nervous energy out, not bottle it up as the lads seemed to do. They would sit around all quiet yet fidgety, worrying about the game ahead. Of course, you've got to focus your mind on the match and different players like to prepare in different ways, but I think you need to be able to have a laugh and a joke before the three-minute bell goes and suddenly you're out there on the pitch. Wrighty would have his music blaring out and gee himself up by dancing around while I'd try to encourage a bit of banter amongst the lads to calm the nerves. I think our off-the-wall approach brought a few of the lads out of their shells and if that in turn enables them to express themselves more on the pitch, it can only be a positive thing. We certainly started the season on a high and looked as though we meant business.

The target from day one was to get a place in Europe; we didn't want to be scrapping around at the bottom of the table worrying about relegation. The fact that the club had resisted the temptation to cash in on the talents of people like Ferdinand and Lampard was encouraging, not just for the fans but everyone at the club, and it showed that West Ham weren't prepared to settle for the role of also-rans. With the experience and know-how that myself and Wrighty – and a bit later, Paolo Di Canio – could add to the side, there was no reason why we couldn't go places this season. From a personal point of view, I was looking forward to playing alongside Rio, who is a fantastic talent, brilliant on the ball and a good reader of the game for someone so young. He'd already made great strides and he'll be an England regular for years to come. Yet while he's such a confident and gifted footballer, I was surprised how quiet he was on the pitch; well, he was until I arrived on the scene, that is. I remember being the same as him at that age but playing alongside the likes of Russell Osman, John Burridge, Jimmy Case and Terry Hurlock, who were always talking to you, encouraging and generally passing on advice, and taught me a lot about the value of communication on the field. I think Harry hoped that my presence alongside Rio would bring him out his shell, and he's certainly a lot noisier now than he was when I first joined the club. By adding things like that to his game, he's rapidly becoming the complete player everyone at West Ham believed he would be.

We seemed to strike up a good understanding virtually from the off and to keep three clean sheets in our first three league games of the season was an encouraging sign. I'd only played in a couple of pre-season games for the Hammers, having signed too late to join them on their tour of Scotland. But I'd worked hard during my last few weeks at Liverpool and felt good as I made my league debut for West Ham in the opening game of the season at Hillsborough. Ironically, I made my debuts for both Southampton and Liverpool against Sheffield Wednesday, so this completed a rather unique hat-trick. But, while I'd never enjoyed that much success on my previous visits to Hillsborough, this time we came away with a 1–0 win thanks to a goal from Wrighty ten minutes from time. The perfect start. Unfortunately, Wrighty took a knock in training during the next week and missed the visit of Manchester United to Upton Park the following Saturday.

It was my home debut, but that didn't matter to the media who were only really interested in one thing: the first away performance of David Beckham following his sending off in the World Cup against Argentina. Even the United debut of £12.6 million striker Dwight Yorke took a backseat because everyone was talking about Beckham and the reception the United player, who originally hailed from the East End, was going to get from the Hammers' fans. There was what can only be described as a hate campaign going on against Beckham and, although what he did at France 98 was both stupid and petulant, the reaction of supporters all over the country was totally over the top. Nobody deserves to take that much stick.

I was more concerned with keeping tabs on former Villa striker Yorke and I was pleased with my performance against a player I have always admired and rate as one of my most difficult opponents. He's such a live-wire, a bit like Wrighty really, and you're never quite sure where he's going to pop up or what he's going to try next. But on this occasion he had a quiet game by his standards and we kept another clean sheet after I'd got away with a handball offence as I attempted to get to a deep Ryan Giggs cross. You need a bit of good fortune from time to time and on this occasion luck was on my side. Not that there was anything lucky about the Man of the Match award which I was happy to collect afterwards, you understand!

All modesty aside, I'd settled in pretty well and after another clean sheet against Coventry I was named West Ham's Player of the Month by the supporters which was a nice feeling. When you join a new club you always want to get off to a good start and get the fans on your side and, thankfully, that was the case as we were unbeaten in three and my confidence was sky high. As for the fourth game of the season, that was a different matter entirely. Even now I can't explain what happened in the home game against Wimbledon, who came back from three goals down to win 4–3 in a bizarre match best forgotten. It was a typical Wimbledon performance, bombing us from all angles, and we buckled under the pressure. While I was happy to take the accolades for my previous perform-ances, it was only right and proper that I took my fair share of the blame for this Upton Park debacle. Harry, understandably, went ballistic. There was more bad news for Wrighty when he later found out that he was heading for trouble with the FA for revealing a T-shirt supporting the striking Essex firemen as he celebrated his two goals. You'd think the authorities would have more important things to deal with, wouldn't you?

It was important we got that defeat out of our system as soon as possible, especially as we were playing my old club Liverpool a few days later. It was another tough, personal test for me because I was up against the brilliant Michael Owen but, just as we'd managed to keep Yorke quiet against United, we put the shackles on Michael who was asked to play a lone role up front. We held on for a 2–1 win that day, but were brought down to earth with a bump when we travelled to Northampton Town's new Sixfield Stadium the following Wednesday and lost 2–0 in the Worthington Cup. Although we beat our Second Division opponents 1–0 in the return leg, we were out of the cup. Worse still, I picked up an Achilles injury in the first game at Northampton and was forced to sit out the next few games which was frustrating, but at least the problem wasn't serious.

The fact that we could play so well and beat a side like Liverpool one day, then lose to a team like Northampton a few days later, was a bit worrying. To be successful, you have to be consistent and we couldn't seem to string a run of winning matches together. It was something we needed to address. A more pressing matter on Harry Redknapp's agenda at that time, however, concerned the infamous training ground bust-up between John Hartson and Eyal Berkovic. I've seen a few clashes between team-mates in my time, and I've been involved in a few, but by any stretch of the imagination, this was in a different league.

CHAPTER TWELVE

There May Be Trouble Ahead

The first couple of months of my West Ham career had gone pretty well – the Worthington Cup embarrassment against Northampton aside – and without a hint of controversy. But a training ground incident which should have led to little more than an internal investigation suddenly became the subject of a massive public debate. And all because a punter had been allowed into the training ground with a camcorder and had captured the whole thing on film. Nine times out of ten such a confrontation between two team-mates would not have been made public knowledge and would have been dealt with by the manager in the privacy of his own office. Not that I would condone what John Hartson did to Eyal Berkovic that day. There are often scuffles and skirmishes between team-mates, good old-fashioned punch-ups even, but I must admit I had never seen anything quite like this before. Eyal told the papers back home in Israel that John had kicked his head 'like a football', and the description wasn't too far off the mark. But it was the fact that the moment was caught on camera and slowed right down for the purposes of television coverage on Sky which probably made it look worse than it actually was. The newspapers, too, used a series of stills to show the incident step-by-step, so it made it difficult for Harry to play it down, as much as he tried.

It wasn't as if a conflict between the two lads had been brewing beforehand; it was hardly a fair match, after all. It was just one of those heat-of-the-moment things which happen from time to time when you have fiery characters like John around. The fact that it happened to be the biggest bloke at the club seemingly trying to remove the head of the smallest fella from his shoulders didn't really do John any favours. If it had been me on the receiving end of John's boot, then everyone would have laughed. But he was genuinely sorry about what had happened and full of remorse straight afterwards. In fact, he was devastated. He'd lost control for a split second and the consequences were there for all to see once the person who'd filmed the incident had decided to cash-in on his stroke of fortune of being in the right place at the right time. Unfortunately for Eyal, he just happened to be in the wrong place at the wrong time!

I was quite close to the incident, which happened at West Ham's Chadwell Heath ground during a routine training session at the end of September 1998. It all began with John flattening Eyal with a tackle from behind which the little midfielder took exception to. As he went to get up off the ground, Eyal threw out an arm in handbags' style and just caught John, who reacted instantly by kicking out at the Israeli. It looked on film as if 'Hart' had landed his left foot volley full in the face of Eyal but, in actual fact, I think he caught him on the shoulder before flicking the side of his face. If John's boot had got him straight in the kisser, I doubt Eyal would have got up so quickly. Maybe the intention was there, but that was the way Johnny was playing at the time and he missed! As soon as it happened the players rushed over and I stepped in first to check that Eyal was okay and then usher John out of the way to avoid any further confrontation. It was all over in a flash but, predictably, the repercussions rumbled on for days, weeks even, following the release of the camcorder footage to the papers. All of them tried to build it up into a personal feud between the two players, which wasn't really the case.

John apologised to Eyal, they kissed and made up and that was the end of it as far as we were concerned. After a few days, things were back to normal and it was all forgotten about – although not by a couple of Northampton players who used the incident as the basis for a goal celebration with the scorer going down on his knees and another player kicking him in the head. Nice one! Me and Wrighty had that one up our sleeves, but they beat us to it.

Needless to say, Harry didn't see the funny side of it and had both players in to clear the air once and for all. It didn't really help matters, however, when an interview Eyal had done with a newspaper back home in Tel Aviv reached the hands of the English press and it was all blown up again. Apparently, Eyal was quoted as saying that he would find it difficult to forgive John Hartson.

I found Eyal's attitude a bit sad. One minute he was

happy to be pictured with John, making out they were the best of friends and that what happened on the training field had been forgotten; the next he was squealing to the press back home in Israel that he was an outcast. He was a loner and didn't mix with the lads but, even still, to come out and describe West Ham as a 'pub team' was an absolute disgrace. As for suggesting that we were excluding him because he was a foreigner, that's laugh-able. As everyone knows, we have a lot of foreign players at the club, a number of black players too, but they are all treated exactly the same as if they were born in the East End of London. If Eyal didn't feel as though he fitted in, that's his problem, not ours. I don't think too many people at West Ham shed any tears when he was later sold to Celtic. Not that Harry got rid of him because of any personality clashes; it's just that he was offered good money by another club and the manager considered it good business to let him go. We weren't going to stand in his way.

I don't think the training ground incident had anything to do with Harry's decision to sell John to Wimbledon later in the year either. That was simply down to good business on the boss's part because he was getting £7.5 million for a player he'd signed for £4 million less not that long ago. We were sorry to see Johnny go because as well being a terrific player he was actually a nice fella and a good character to have around. A bit of a gentle giant, even if he did go round head-butting plant pots and getting himself into trouble as he did around the same time following a night out in Swansea. I can see the headline now: 'CRACK POT MEETS PLANT POT'.

Events on the field were pretty interesting too and

191

after a disappointing run of results, which included a heavy defeat against Blackburn and a home-derby reverse against Charlton, we got back into winning ways with an impressive 3–0 victory away at Newcastle where I found myself up against my old pal Alan Shearer. He wasn't enjoying the best of times at St James' Park, mainly because he was being starved of the service he needs, and you could sense the frustration in his play. He wasn't the same all-action striker I'd been used to playing against, and seemed unusually subdued, often walking around with his head down, which was not like Alan. But I wouldn't go along with the view that he was past his best and that the bad knee injury he'd suffered a few years ago had deprived him of a yard of pace. He was simply playing in an average side which wasn't creating the sort of chances he was accustomed to being supplied with, and he appeared to have become disheartened as a result. It wasn't as if he was missing chances every week; he just wasn't getting the oppor-tunities to miss them in the first place. Alan is still a fantastic goalscorer but, like a lot of the Newcastle players, he seemed a bit short on confidence. He had a goal disallowed in the first half but, apart from that, had a quiet afternoon and didn't cause us too many problems. The scores were level at half-time, but Wrighty grabbed a couple in the second half and, after they'd had Stuart Pearce sent off for a challenge on Trevor Sinclair, we ran out comfortable 3–0 winners.

A week later it was my turn to get on the scoresheet as I registered my first goal for West Ham in a 1–1 draw with Chelsea. And it wasn't the usual Ruddock towering header either. We had a free-kick outside their box and I told young Frankie Lampard to roll the ball to me, confidently telling him that I was going to 'bend a left-footer around the wall and into the bottom corner'. That's exactly what I did. We won our next three games – against Leicester, Derby and Spurs – and we looked to be on a roll; until we went up to Elland Road where it all went pear-shaped. We got hammered 4–0 and I was sent off for the first time as a West Ham player for a challenge on Harry Kewell. It wasn't the best tackle in the world, ever-so-slightly mistimed maybe, but I don't think it was as bad as people made out and certainly not deserving of a red card. A few years ago you'd have got booked and given a ticking off by the referee for a tackle like that, but I got a straight red. I'm not saying my reputation had gone before me, although I'm convinced it has done on occasions in the past, it's just that the rules leave the referees with little or no option to use commonsense. You just don't get the benefit of the doubt any more. In addition to the red card, I picked up eight yellows last season and that's pretty much par for the course for defenders. Any defender, not just me. I blame the people who lay down the laws, not the officials who have to enforce them. Now there's a first, Neil 'Razor' Ruddock, leaping to the defence of the enemy. The only good thing to come out of the dismissal at Elland Road was the fact that, not for the first time in my career, I would be suspended during the Christmas programme. I still managed to make the headlines over the festive period though.

Most of the football club Christmas parties I've attended over the years have been memorable and so was my first one as a West Ham player, but for all the wrong reasons. It all started innocently enough with the lads enjoying a few lunchtime drinks around the bars of

Romford before heading off to a café where we'd arranged to eat before making our way to the party venue. All very civilised; or so we thought. As a member of the so-called organising committee, I was in charge of 'transport and accounts' or, to put it another way, taxis and the kitty. What I didn't have any control over was an incident which had apparently happened outside while I was settling up the tab inside with Ian Wright. My Christmas festivities were cut dramatically short when the police turned up and started quizzing us about a car being damaged, allegedly by a 'black man and a white man' in fancy dress. I asked the police to tell me who the blokes in question were so I could get them out to answer the charges and we could get on with our Christmas celebrations. Which is where it all started going horribly wrong, because they indicated I was one of the suspects, even though I'd been nowhere near the incident in question. The funny thing was that they were looking for people in 1970s gear wearing long, curly black wigs. But as we were all dressed the same in loud jackets and flares, I couldn't see how they could single anyone out. Because I was in reception paying the bill, I was the first person they came across who fitted the description of the 'white man' they were supposedly looking for, and I was whisked off for questioning along with Trevor Sinclair. As Trevor was wearing a bright pink suit at the time, he was a damn-sight easier to spot.

The police reckoned they had got us on CCTV so I said 'Come on then, let's go and have a look at the film'. I thought it would just be a case of going down to the station, looking at the video to prove it wasn't me and walking out again. But it didn't work out that way. When we got to the station they admitted they hadn't any evidence on video, but they'd got the pair of us in their custody by then and duly charged us with 'causing an affray', although my charge was later reduced to 'threatening behaviour'. This all happened at about 6 pm on the Sunday evening and I wasn't let out until about 1 am the next morning, so I missed the whole of the party. Not very amusing, I can tell you, a bit of a nightmare in fact, although I did have to chuckle at one point when I realised I was still holding the kitty and the other lads didn't have any money, so they had to run up a tab. You should have seen the faces of the coppers when I had to empty my pockets!

The reason they kept me in for so long had nothing to do with my behaviour or conduct, it was down to the fact that dear old Trevor was too drunk to give a statement until later in the evening and I had to wait until he was sober enough to give his evidence before I could give mine. Thanks, Trev. Eventually they let us go and when my father-in-law Paul came to pick us up at about 1 am, the press were crawling all round the police station wanting to know what had happened. Who tipped the media off, I'll never know!

It was rumoured afterwards that the girl involved in the incident, which basically involved someone rolling on the bonnet of her car and someone else, allegedly, throwing a bottle, had called the police and then decided to make a few quid by contacting the media. Needless to say, it was all over the papers that I'd been involved in a boozy row, but I was determined to clear my name and prove my innocence which, after a number of court appearances before Romford Magistrates, I did. What I found particularly annoying was that, when the story came out originally, it was all over the papers and on the television and radio, yet when I was cleared in court, they printed about two paragraphs saying that I was innocent. But that's the media for you.

I was never at any stage worried about being found guilty but I must admit that, the morning after it happened, I was more than a little concerned what Harry Redknapp would be thinking – and what action he would take – after the news had filtered back to him. I had only been with the club a few months and I didn't want him to think I had abused the faith he had shown in me when he signed me from Liverpool in the summer. I knew I hadn't done anything to bring shame on myself or the club, but you know how stories of this nature can be blown out of all proportion before the true version eventually comes to light.

Obviously Harry was keen to get to the bottom of this as soon as possible and both myself and Trevor went in to see him the next morning to give him our side of the story. As soon as I walked in Harry started effing and blinding, calling me all the names under the sun before I managed to tell him the incident was nothing to do with me. He'd heard various stories ('There's no smoke without fire, Razor') and when I told him I wasn't the guilty party he called the lads together for a meeting to find out who was to blame. I refused to name the person responsible and after a while Harry calmed down and, within a day or so, things had got back to normal. It wasn't a nice feeling, however, having to go in and see him like a naughty schoolboy, but the worst bit about it all was that I had to take my kids to school every day knowing that people were thinking their father was a trouble-maker. Well, they now know the truth.

As it transpired, my case was thrown out of court even

before all the evidence had been heard because the stories of the two prosecution witnesses, the girl who was driving the car and her boyfriend, simply didn't match up. In fact, they were from Land's End to John O'Groats apart. They made themselves look a laughing stock because they couldn't get the simplest of facts right. For example, one of them reckoned I was three feet away when I supposedly threw a bottle, whereas the other one stated I was 50 yards away when I threw a glass. Yet the truth of the matter was I was nowhere to be seen. A classic case of mistaken identity, you might say. No case to answer, end of story. But even though my name was cleared, it was still annoying that I'd had to go through months of investiga-tions and dealings with solicitors over something that really shouldn't have come to court in the first place. If it had been two normal members of the public supposedly involved, rather than two professional footballers, I doubt it would have even made it as far as the police station, let alone a court of law. These sort of things happen three or four times a night in a place like Romford and nothing ever gets done about it. Because we happened to be Trevor Sinclair and Neil Ruddock of West Ham United Football Club, suddenly it's a different matter. It was a waste of taxpayers' money, although my legal costs were all covered because the case was thrown out. Big thanks to my solicitor Stephen Welfare of Royds Treadwell.

Having had to contend with all the hassles surrounding the Christmas party incident, I just wanted to get back to playing football after serving my three-match suspension for the sending off at Leeds over the holiday period. Some holiday! I made my return in the FA Cup third round tie against Swansea which, on paper, looked like a comfortable game in which to ease myself back into first team action. Having already been knocked out of the Worthington Cup by Northampton, I should have known better than to think Swansea wouldn't come and make life difficult for us on our own patch. In fact, it took a last minute goal from Julian Dicks, of all people, to save our blushes after they had taken the lead and threatened to cause the shock of the round. I don't think it was that we underestimated them, we just didn't play on the day and only got out of jail with almost the last kick of the game. But at least Dicksy's goal gave us another chance to make amends in the replay, and provided him with a rare moment of glory after going to hell and back with his troublesome knee. Most players would have given up hope of recovering from such a crippling injury, but my old Liverpool team-mate is made of stronger stuff than that. It was great to see him in action and leading the charge when the team was struggling, even though his retirement from the game has been on the cards for some time. His fighting spirit is incredible and I don't think many other players would have been able to do what he has done after undergoing so much surgery. It shows real determination. He could have retired and taken a lot of money, but he wanted to keep on playing for West Ham. Even though he wasn't able to train properly, whenever he was called upon he never let you down. Dicksy is a Hammers' legend and it was great for the fans and the team to see him back. I always loved playing alongside him at Liverpool because he gives the whole team a lift with his enthusiasm and commit-ment. Just having him out there makes you feel an inch taller.

Another boost for the club at a time when we were

finding victories, draws even, hard to come by, was the signing of the man everyone was calling the 'Italian hothead', Paolo Di Canio. Now Harry's track record with foreigners is probably not the best (remember Marco Boogers and more recently Javier Margas, who did a runner back to Chile because he didn't like the soft pitches?) and a lot of people suggested he was taking a massive gamble on the former Sheffield Wednesday player who fell out of love with the Owls after serving his ban for 'violently' shoving referee Paul Alcock to the ground! Personally I reckoned that a million pounds amounted to loose change for a player with his skill, even if he is prone to flying off the handle, shall we say. And seeing as Harry had £7.5 million burning a hole in his pocket after selling John Hartson to Wimbledon – the sale of the season – why not take a bit of a punt? Di Canio is a fantastic player and we soon discovered that he has a wonderful sense of humour too.

Soon after Paul Alcock had fallen to the ground in instalments following the gentlest of shoves by the Italian, myself and Wrighty staged an action replay of the comical incident as part of our goal celebration in a 1–0 win against Southampton. Basically, after Ian had scored, he ran over to me and showed me an imaginary red card, at which point I gave him a shove and he went down like a sack of spuds. Everyone thought it was hilarious, but even though referee Uriah Rennie had turned a blind eye to the celebration, the suits at the FA apparently didn't see the funny side of it. We didn't get fined or anything like that, but the fact that the powers-that-be had even considered making an issue of it just about summed them up. Supporters everywhere came up to us afterwards and said it was the best celebration they'd seen and I can remember my old Liverpool team-mate Jamie Redknapp making a point of calling me on the mobile after the game and he was literally crying with laughter. It was a bit of fun, nothing else.

Which brings me to the arrival of Di Canio at West Ham because his opening gambit when he walked into the dressing room to meet the lads for the first time was to point an accusing finger at me and Wrighty and say: 'Hey, you two, you taker de piss or what?' It certainly broke the ice and endeared him to his new team-mates straight-away. He's been a diamond ever since, on and off the field. Talking to Paolo about the Hillsborough histrionics of Mr Alcock also reminded us of an amusing incident which occurred at the start of the season when the same official visited the club to talk to the players about some of the new rules which were being introduced.

He waffled on about this change and that change but said the thing they were most concerned about was players diving, and how they were going to clamp down on people like David Ginola and Emile Heskey – who were mentioned specifically by Alcock – and issue yellow cards for 'ungentlemanly conduct'. How ironic that Mr Alcock should prove to be one of the finest exponents of this particular art. The amazing thing about it all was how he later threatened to sue because he'd injured his back and claimed he was suffering from stress. Unbelievable. It's little wonder he's no longer refereeing in the Premiership because nobody could take him seriously after that; he'd become a laughing stock. It was the best dive since Greg Louganis.

The incident involving Alcock and Paolo confirmed what we already knew about the fiery Italian; that he was a volcano waiting to erupt. Which is why, a few weeks earlier when we played his former club Sheffield Wednesday on the opening day of the season, Harry Redknapp had pulled me to one side before my West Ham debut and told me to wind Di Canio up and put him off his game. He was the sort of player who would 'lose it', as they say, and the instructions were to give him a bit of stick, rough him up if you like, and see how he reacted. He didn't exactly blow up that day, but we did manage to keep him pretty quiet and came away with a 1–0 win as a result. If a player's more concerned about getting even, he's less likely to concentrate on the things he's good at, and we all know how good Paolo can be if you let him play. That sort of thing goes on all the time and, although you never set out with the intention of hurting someone physically, you can affect them mentally.

It happened to me on several occasions when I was younger and my temper was a bit suspect. Like Paolo, I've calmed down a lot as I've got older, but when I was in my early 20s I had a short fuse and was fair game for a wind-up. I'm sure managers used to tell certain players in their side to try and rattle me and get me to react, as I did from time to time. The Craig Short incident, during my Southampton days, was a typical case of an opponent winding me up during a game to get me sent off; and I fell for it hook, line and sinker. David Speedie was another player who was a master at getting to opponents with a constant stream of verbals and digs from behind. One minute he'd be pinching you, the next standing on your toes at a corner – and he was only a little so and so. I used to hate playing against him at the time but now, whenever we meet up at a football function I'll give him a hug and we'll have a laugh about what a horrible piece of work he was.

That sort of thing goes on all the time and is part and parcel of the game at all levels. But professionals never set out to cause serious damage; let them know you're there early on with a good, hard tackle, but nothing too dangerous. I remember an occasion, again at The Dell, when we were playing Sheffield Wednesday and the manager at the time, Chris Nicholl, told myself and Alan Shearer – the 'bruise brothers' as they called us – to unsettle their keeper, Chris Woods, the first chance we got. Sure enough, when our first corner was lobbed in towards the six-yard box, inviting Woods to come for it, both me and Shearer went flying in with what you would diplomatically call 'powerful aerial challenges'. There was an almighty collision which resulted in Woods lying face down on the floor and Shearer staggering about like a boxer on his last legs after the keeper had punched him in the head instead of the ball. Thankfully, I walked away unscathed.

You've got to have physical contact and you've got to have physical players in your team who can look after themselves, and others. Every successful team has got them. Of course, you have to complement the workers with the playmakers, in the same way as you combine youth and experience, and I happen to believe we've got a pretty good blend at West Ham.

CHAPTER THIRTEEN

Changing Man

After being knocked out of both cup competitions by lower league opposition and going through a dodgy spell in the league which threatened to undermine our European ambitions, I think some of the lads needed a bit of a lift and the arrival of Paolo Di Canio, for all his faults, certainly helped do that. So did the promising debut of the latest young star to roll off the Hammers' production line, teenage sensation Joe Cole. Believe me, this boy is special and is going all the way. Harry had so much confidence and faith in young Joe that he didn't hesitate in handing him his first team debut, when he was still only 17, at Old Trafford of all places. We suffered another bad defeat, 4–1, at the hands of Manchester United but the one bright spot was the appearance of Joe at half-time and the way he rose to the occasion over the next 45 minutes. He was superb and totally unfazed by the whole occasion, as Harry had predicted.

Wherever I've been in my career I've seen brilliant young talent emerging. At Spurs there was Sol Campbell, at Southampton Alan Shearer and at Liverpool both

Robbie Fowler and Michael Owen. I've witnessed at first hand the impact they have made and their amazing progress at the highest level, and Joe has definitely got the ability to go on and achieve as much, if not more than the four England stars I've just mentioned. I'd be happy to be blessed with 50 per cent of Joe's ability on the ball. He's got unbelievable skill, with all the confidence in the world to go with it, and I'm sure that, injuries permitting, Joe will go all the way to the top. He's a lovely lad who seems to take everything in his stride, a lot like Michael Owen, and he's definitely not one of these cocky kids who gets ideas above his station. He pays a lot of attention to the older players around him, even though he can show us a thing or two with the ball, and providing he keeps listening to and learning from the coaching staff and senior pros, there's no end to what he can achieve. It speaks volumes for the club and its fantastic youth policy that Joe is not the only teenager setting Upton Park alight. But he is the best. Harry thinks the world of him, and it's easy to see why; Joe's either going to save him or make him an absolute fortune.

Because of the cash situation at West Ham, the club has relied heavily on the youth system and it's paid off with interest. Rio Ferdinand and Frank Lampard have already established themselves and young Joe is on the first rung of the ladder. There are plenty of others coming through as well and you only have to look at the way the youngsters destroyed everyone on their way to winning the FA Youth Cup last season to see the potential. Midfielder Michael Carrick, in particular, is a player who is exciting the pants off the youth coaches at Upton Park and great things are expected of him. So the future looks very promising.

The immediate future, however, did not look so good for me after I picked up a hamstring injury early on in the 4–0 home defeat by Sheffield Wednesday, just a few days after we'd been dumped out of the FA Cup by Swansea in a replay at the Vetch Field. When we then suffered another 4–0 home battering, this time by Arsenal, the European hopes we'd harboured since the opening day of the season were beginning to fade and die, as they say in these parts. I'll say one thing for West Ham – when we lose, we do it in style, as we did on a number of occasions last season. It was no laughing matter though, certainly not at that stage of the season, when we desperately needed to regroup, go back to basics and get some more points on the board if we were to achieve our original aim of getting into Europe. We showed a lot of character at that time to turn things around and a 1–0 win at Stamford Bridge was arguably our best performance of the season. Nobody really expected us to get a result against a Chelsea side that was playing some great stuff at the time, but the victory gave us a lot of confidence for the run-in.

Even when things were going against us for a spell, the atmosphere at the club was still positive and the training ground was still an enjoyable place to be. When you've got people like Wrighty and John Moncur, the craziest man in football, around the place, the lads are always going to have a smile on their face irrespective of what is happening on the pitch at weekends.

In addition to being a fantastic player who can lift people with his enthusiasm and passion for the game, Wrighty is one of the game's great characters and, although we never saw eye-to-eye as opponents, we became good friends when we teamed up in the

England squad a few years ago and we've since cemented that relationship after becoming colleagues at West Ham. He came into professional football late and I think that must have something to do with the incredible appetite and zest he still has for the game. He's brilliant to have around the dressing room, although if you've got a bit of a headache or you're not feeling too energetic, Wrighty is the last person you want to see first thing in the morning because he's *always* loud and lively. As Harry Redknapp has gone on record as saying, the dressing room at West Ham was a bit quiet until me and Wrighty arrived. Before my first game for the club at the start of last season I turned up with the biggest ghetto-blaster in the world; so big that John Hartson thought the case I was carrying on my shoulders was a set of golf clubs! I didn't tell Harry what I was doing but once I walked in the dressing room, slammed it down on the treatment table and turned the music up full pelt, he looked at me and gave me wink which said, 'Nice one Razor, well done'. It certainly got everyone going, especially Wrighty who was dancing on the table in the middle of the room, banging on the ceiling and generally going nuts. Wrighty's such a brilliant character to have around and he had me in stitches before the start of the season when we were playing in a friendly against local side Purfleet. They had a big centre-half playing for them who insisted on giving Wrighty a hard time throughout the match, thinking he was jack the lad trying to wind up one of the game's biggest wind-up merchants. At one point, after they had exchanged a few verbals, the defender turned to Wrighty and said, 'You've got a problem, you have.' Quick as a flash, Wrighty replied,

'Look mate, the only problem I've got is whether to buy a black Ferrari or a red one!'

When Wrighty retires from football, I'm sure a step into the world of films won't be far away. If Vinnie Jones can take Hollywood by storm, then I'm sure there's a place for Ian Wright on the big screen.

Another one of the West Ham lads who wouldn't look out of place on the stage is John Moncur, who is the life and soul of the club, as he was when I first met him at Tottenham. I could probably fill a book about some of his crazy stunts alone. When Paul Gascoigne says that 'Monc' is the funniest person he has met in football, then it gives you some idea of what he's like. Let me give you a few examples. Steve Lomas had a house-warming party not so long back and all the lads were invited to do a turn but, because he was too embarrassed to sing, John decided to do the 'Full Monty' instead. Needless to say, he went the whole way, but the funniest thing was when he lifted his hat to reveal everything and fell off the back of the stage with his legs in the air and his tackle in full view of the mixed audience, cutting his eye open in the process as everyone fell about laughing. But then John has always been prone to getting his kit off. Like the time we turned up for training one freezing cold morning and, because we'd all put double kit on to combat the weather, there was nothing left for him when he arrived late. Undeterred, he came running out onto the training pitch, in the rain and the snow, wearing nothing but his football boots and a pair of socks, with about 200 supporters – together with Harry Redknapp – looking on in disbelief. John will do anything for a laugh and is a fantastic bloke to have around to lift the spirits. Not that one of the street performers in Covent Garden appreciated his sense of humour one evening when the lads were on the town. This entertainer was attracting quite a crowd with his fire-eating display when suddenly 'Monc' appeared from nowhere with a fire extinguisher from a nearby bar and destroyed the act. But while John loves a laugh, he takes his football seriously and is a very gifted performer. Although he wasn't a regular in the team last season, his spirits never dropped and you could always count on him when he was called into the side. He's got great skills and is an ideal West Ham player.

We managed to string a few decent results together as the season drew to a nail-biting climax to keep us in contention for Europe, although we were kept guessing all the way to the end of the season as to whether fifth place would be good enough to qualify automatically for the UEFA Cup, or whether we would have to do so via the Intertoto Cup. Surely the rules about this should have been laid down at the start of the season, not right at the end?

All we could do was keep battling away and hope for the best, and things seemed to be going pretty much according to plan after we beat Derby 5–1, with Yours Truly getting on the scoresheet. Mind you, despite the eventual scoreline, we did need our giant keeper Shaka Hislop to be in his best form because, without him, we would have been 3–0 down inside the first 15 minutes. He pulled off some magnificent saves and gave us the platform to go on and win the game after a dodgy start, which probably explains why he was named man of the match even though the team ended up with five goals. But then we have become accustomed to the big man – 'Shaka flip-flop' as I like to call him – producing performances like that week in, week out and it's hard to imagine how Newcastle could let him go without a fight. My old mate Alan Shearer couldn't believe it either.

To get him on a free transfer was brilliant for the club and he showed everyone what a great, all-round keeper he is by being named Player of the Season by the fans, who love him. The only problem we have with Shaka is understanding some of the instructions he barks out from behind us in his Trinidad and Tobagan accent. You know when he's coming for the ball though and, because of the size of him, it makes sense to keep out of the way. He's so laid-back, typically Caribbean, and he's a very popular player at the club because he's got such a lovely manner.

So things were looking up once more and another victory in our next match, against London rivals Spurs, put us within reach of that European place. It was a fast and furious game with tackles flying in all over the park and it was no real surprise when referee Uriah Rennie sent off John Moncur for what someone in the press aptly described as 'a scything lunge' on Mauricio Taricco as tempers flared. John was really fired up for this one, as all the lads were, and we had to smile when he left the field, with his clenched fists raised in the air, to a hero's farewell from the West Ham fans. It was typical of the fighting spirit that was running through the side. There was so much at stake and we weren't going to give up the ghost without a scrap.

So, with just three games to go, the signs were good; until we played Leeds in the next match at Upton Park, that is. Now we've all seen referees lose control of matches from time to time, but on this occasion Rob Harris lost the plot ... completely. Not only did we concede five goals, at home too, but we had three players sent off for next-to-nothing offences and the game turned into an absolute farce because of the official's incompetence. But it wasn't just the sendings off that he got wrong; he was off the mark with virtually every other decision all afternoon. He gave corners instead of goal-kicks, awarded throw-ins the wrong way and generally made a complete hash of everything. It got to the point where, even though tempers were getting frayed and players were getting sent off left, right and centre, those left on the field, on both sides, just stood laughing at the official whose performance was beyond a joke. We were down to eight men by the time Mr Harris had sent off Steve Lomas for 'serious foul play' in the last minute, having already dished out red cards to Shaka Hislop (for bringing a man down when defenders were behind him) and Ian Wright for an alleged off-the-ball incident which nobody saw apart from the linesman – sorry, assistant referee. I think it's fair to say that, having seemingly accepted the decision for what it was (crap!) Wrighty also lost the plot as he made his way off the field after just 17 minutes. At one point he appeared to be walking away from the scene calmly, but then something must have snapped, the red mist descended and all hell broke loose as he tried to get to the ref. I'm pretty sure he wouldn't have laid a finger on the Mr Harris, not after the trouble Di Canio had caused for himself earlier in the season, but he was in such a rage that he could have said something out of place and got into all sorts of bother, so Trevor Sinclair stepped in and dragged him away.

I've seen Wrighty lose his rag before, but this time he went big time. He must have been out of control because, as it later emerged, he barged his way into the referee's locked dressing room and smashed up the television set in his rage. The thing is, the players didn't know anything about the incident until the next morning when we read the papers. Wrighty was so incensed that, instead of getting changed, and waiting around until the end of the game, he walked straight out of the ground and went home, which was probably a wise thing to do given his state of mind at the time. If he'd stayed at the ground, the press would have been on his case and he may well have talked himself into another disrepute charge. The papers were full of allegations about him trashing the dressing room and damaging stuff belonging to the referee. But the only thing that got smashed was the television set, which was owned by the club anyway. Even so, the incident cost Wrighty a three-match ban to take effect at the start of the following season and a £17,500 fine. I'm sure, once he'd calmed down, he regretted his actions but at the time he felt he had been harshly treated and we all saw how he reacted. The annoying thing about that game was that the referee could have cost us a place in Europe.

But while we considered the official to be at fault against Leeds, it was the players who had to shoulder the blame for the next setback to our European hopes a week later at Goodison Park. Quite frankly, we were abysmal against an Everton side that had been fighting against relegation all season and we were hammered 6–0 on an embarrassing afternoon for all of us in a West Ham shirt. It seemed ridiculous for a team in our position in the league to concede 11 goals in two games at such a crucial stage of the season and we knew we only had one more match, against Middlesbrough on the final day, to put things right. We did just that and, once Frank Lampard had put us ahead against Boro' after just four minutes, there was only going to be one winner. Not for the first time during the season, young Frank confirmed what I had felt from day one as a West Ham team-mate: he's one of the best goalscoring midfielders I've ever worked with and, like Rio Ferdinand, he's going to be a permanent fixture in the England squad for years to come. Frank is arguably *the* best finisher at the club, although Ian Wright might disagree, and you have to admire him for the way he's overcome a lot of barracking from some West Ham fans who reckoned he was only in the team because his old man, Frank senior, is Harry's number two. That was never the case and I think it's unfair for fans to level that at him; he has always been in the team on merit and has more than justified his inclusion over the last couple of seasons. I'd love to see him playing alongside Jamie Redknapp in the England midfield because, with Jamie's passing ability and young Frank's nose for goal, I think they'd be an ideal combination. Frank's proved a lot of people wrong – with his actions on the field and not his words in the press – and I'm delighted for him, especially as he's such a level-headed lad who's a pleasure to work with. A bit too good looking for my liking, though.

His early goal in that final league game against Middlesbrough was just what we needed and when Marc Keller, Trevor Sinclair and Paolo Di Canio rattled in three more we knew we had achieved our aim of qualifying for the Intertoto Cup. The way we celebrated – a conga here, a group slide there – you'd have thought we'd won the treble instead of Manchester United. But to finish fifth in the Premiership was a magnificent achievement and, with the squad Harry has brilliantly assembled at Upton Park, there's no reason why we can't build on that success. With the addition of people like Stuart Pearce, Paulo Wanchope and Igor Stimac – plus a brilliant crop of youngsters on the fringe of the first team – I'm confident we've got a group of players capable of bringing a trophy of some description back to the East End of London for the first time since the early eighties.

We were also boosted by the return of Javier Margas who, having done a runner back to Chile because of family problems and the fact that he didn't like the soft pitches in England during the winter months, apparently, finally decided he wanted to make a go of things at Upton Park. Everyone thought he had gone for good when he went home for Christmas and didn't show up again for months, but since his return he has shown his internat-ional class and added even more strength in depth to what Harry has developed into an impressive first team squad. We told Javier that, because West Ham had had trouble with foreign players in recent years, he should do something to assure the fans of his commitment. So the next day he turned up for training with a bloody great British Bulldog tattooed on his arm. Not just a transfer, but the real McCoy. And more recently he dyed his hair claret and blue to show the fans his heart was in the club. Crazy man, but a smashing fella who makes up quite a cosmopolitan dressing room with the likes of Wanchope (Costa Rican), Di Canio (Italian) and Keller (French). The foreigners at West Ham are all good lads and very much part of the West Ham 'family'. The London boys have even got them eating pie and mash, and jellied eels.

I think I'd settled in pretty well too and, after playing 30-odd games in my first season for West Ham I was looking forward to building on that promising start and, having worked hard during the summer, I reported back for the 1999–2000 campaign in good shape. Which was a good job really because our involvement in the Intertoto Cup meant we were going virtually straight into competitive games, after a couple of run-outs against local sides. Normally you get five or six weeks of playing friendlies, or going away on tour, but there was no such luxury for us as we were drawn to play the Finnish side Jokerit in our first qualifying game. Getting into the UEFA Cup had been our ambition from the start of the previous season, so we were all in determined mood from day one; no messing around and straight down to business. Our football may not have been as fluent as it might have been – we were understandably ring rusty so early in the season – but the attitude was spot on and we had a fairly comfortable passage against the Finns which set up a second qualifying tie against Heerenveen from Holland, who promised to be a tougher proposition altogether.

It was in the away leg against Jokerit that I picked up an injury when I stretched going into a tackle and tweaked a hamstring. I didn't think it was too serious at the time, although I needed a massage afterwards, and the following day the back of my leg was badly bruised. In hindsight, I should have come off as soon as I felt the muscle cramp up, but I decided to see the game through and paid the penalty in the first leg of the Heerenveen tie when the hamstring went completely, ruling me out for six weeks which was very frustrating and bitterly disappoint-ing so early in the season. As soon as it went, I remember thinking 'here we go again' because the same sort of thing had happened to me a couple of times towards the end of my Liverpool career. It was a case of deja vu and, having got myself fit for the new season, I had to face up to the prospect of a few weeks' rest followed by another pre-season slog, effectively. Unlike some players who are more naturally fit, I have to work hard to regain my fitness after injury, mainly because of my size and build, and that was a pretty demoralising thought as we hadn't even begun the new league campaign by then. But at least the lads came through against the Dutch team and then produced a fantastic performance in the away leg against Metz, winning the game 3–1 after losing the home leg 1–0. We had felt all along that we should have qualified for the UEFA Cup automatically so it was satisfying to reach the first round proper, even if we did have to do it the hard way.

As things turned out, playing in so many competitive games so early on probably helped us in the long run because we began the Premiership season in great form and by the end of August we were sitting pretty in fourth place after winning three league games and drawing one. Mind you, as much as you want the team to do well when you're not playing, it was frustrating watching from the sidelines as the lads got off to a flyer. I was jealous of what they were doing, what they were achieving without me, and I desperately wanted to be part of things, especially with the UEFA Cup campaign starting for real with a first round tie against Osijek from Croatia. I felt as though I was missing out and, of course, there's always the doubt in the back of your mind when the team is playing so well that you might not get your place back. Especially as Harry Redknapp had been out and bought Igor Stimac from Derby because of the injury crisis he was faced with. In addition to me, Rio Ferdinand, Ian Pearce and then Stuart Pearce had also picked up injuries.

The injury to Stuart, a broken leg, was particularly cruel because he had been brilliant in the games he had played for us since joining the club from Newcastle just after the start of the season. He has got such tremendous passion for the game and always gives 100 per cent, and more, every time he crosses that white line. It was typical of him that when he was injured in the league game against Watford he refused to be stretchered off the field even though he must have known the injury was serious. I'm sure he would have played on if they'd let him and his attitude at the time was 'It's only broken; I've still got one good leg'. Fantastic.

The fans had taken to him straightaway which was totally understandable because he's such a committed player, like former Upton Park favourite Julian Dicks who was sadly forced to retire because of injury. With both of them, what you see is what you get. Newcastle boss Bobby Robson found it incredible that an influential player of Stuart's stature was allowed to leave Newcastle, but their loss was definitely our gain. He stepped into the side as if he'd been wearing the claret and blue for years and it was brilliant for him to get a recall to the England side at the age of 37; he's a terrific example to us all. It certainly made me think that perhaps I could resurrect my international career and add to my solitary England cap. He's proved that, under Kevin Keegan and irrespective of age, anything is possible. I've had my fair share of tear-ups with Stuart over the years, but I've never had anything but the utmost respect for the man – you will struggle to find a more dedicated and passionate player anywhere in the country; in world football, in fact. I've certainly felt a few of his bone-crunching tackles, but he's always been one of my favourite players and is someone I still look up to.

By comparison with Stuart's injury, my problems were fairly minor but I still knew I would have to battle to get my place back because Stimac had arrived at the club in the meantime and immediately proved what a class act he is. But I've had competition for my place before, like the time Liverpool went out and bought John Scales and Phil Babb, so I knew what to expect. I had no divine right to walk straight back into the team, so it was nice to return to the side alongside the Croatian international in time for the Osijek tie; albeit as a substitute in the first instance. Having come through a couple of reserve games – which I approached as if they were top-of-the-table league games – I was just glad to be back involved with the first team again; training, playing and generally feeling part of things once more after weeks of frustration in the gym and on the treatment table. For that I have the physio staff at the club to thank – John Green, Johnny Byrne and Josh Collins – who were fantastic to me. They worked me hard and pushed me to the limits at times to get me back into shape and, while I might have hated them for punishing me from time to time, I was full of gratitude and respect for the work they did with me. And that's exactly what they did; work *with* me. There's nothing worse than physiotherapists setting you a training or rehabilitation programme and then just leaving you to it because, as every professional athlete knows, it can be difficult to motivate yourself and push yourself when left to your own devices. The three boys were brilliant though and did everything I did, and more, to keep me going through the tough days and put me back on the road to fitness. When you can see the pain on their faces, you appreciate the fact that they are pushing themselves to the limit too; and all for my benefit. That was never the case at Liverpool where the physios simply told you to do this, do that, and basically left you alone to get on with it. That was no good to me. I need to be pushed and that's what John and the boys did, day in, day out. Top men.

Getting my general fitness back was one thing, but regaining match fitness is the all-important thing, so I was delighted to get 30 minutes under my belt in the away leg against Osijek. Scoring a goal in the 3–0 win, with my right foot as well(!), was an added bonus and I gather the television cameras showed exactly what that goal meant to me. It was only a tap-in from a few yards out, and perhaps the opposition wasn't up to much, but it was such a great feeling of relief more than anything. To me, that was the best goal scored in Europe this season. I'm not exactly sure what I was doing in that position; I think we'd had a corner a few minutes before and I was still thinking about making my way back to our half. It meant a lot, though, because I was desperate to prove to people that I was fit, committed and, more importantly, that I was still a good player. The same applied when I played in those two reserves games beforehand because, when you're playing against young lads in the main, you stand out and people are watching to see if you've still got it; and I didn't want to let myself down or let my standards slip. I couldn't bear the thought of people saying 'That Neil Ruddock's lost it' or 'I remember him when he was a good player'. The manager was there too so it was important to show him I was ready for the first team again. I have never, ever, lost faith in my ability – I've always considered myself a good player – but whenever you come back from injury you always feel the need to prove yourself in all departments. And, because your place is no longer guaranteed, it makes you work that much harder to re-establish yourself again; it does me at any rate. The strange thing is that, going into the Osijek game, I was pretty nervous which is unusual for me because I am normally such a confident person. Coming on as sub was a weird experience for me and I was very edgy early on, especially when I made a mess of my first touch; a header which I lost in the floodlights and went straight to their striker who, fortunately for me, wasted a clear cut chance. Within minutes, though, I scored the goal and all the old confidence came flooding back. It did me the power of good, and the feeling was one of pure relief. 'I'm back!' Yet while the game was important to me, it was vital to the team and we turned in a professional performance to put us well in command in the tie.

The visit to that part of the world was also an eye-opener in many other respects because, while we were there, we visited some of the war-torn areas on the Serbian border with Igor acting as our guide. He took us to visit some of his friends who lived in places that had been destroyed in the war, and to see the poverty and devastation at first hand had a profound effect on all the lads; me in particular. It made you feel physically sick to think of what those people had been through and how they were now forced to live their lives. Whole villages had been wiped out and we heard some terrible stories of the mass killings that had gone on; it was like something out of a shocking war film I'd only ever seen at the cinema or on television. I'm glad we went though and I think the people appreciated our visit; especially seeing

Igor, who is a hero in his homeland where, I believe, he owns a number of nightclubs.

Seeing sights of that appalling nature makes you realise how lucky we are; not just as professional footballers but people in general living in a country like England where we are not subjected to anything like that. It was horrific and you wonder how something like that can be allowed to go on in today's world. After all, it was only an hour and 20-minute flight away from the UK. The experience has changed my outlook on so many things. What struck me was the friendliness of the people who made us feel so welcome and I think they appreciated our visit and our performance in the match itself; even though their team lost.

A few days after the European trip I discovered that I would be starting the next Premiership match against Arsenal – Bergkamp, Suker, Kanu, Overmars and the like. What a test that was going to be, but the fact that Harry had enough faith to play me against opposition of such calibre, even though I'd only had 30 minutes of first team action, was another confidence booster for me. I was doubly determined to play well and not let the manager, or the fans, down – and I'd like to think that was how it turned out. It was a massive match against one of the best teams in Europe and to get a result like we did – a 2–1 win with their goal coming late on - was the best feeling in the world; like winning a cup final. Harry is brilliant going into games like that because, whilst he recognises the quality of the opposition and leaves the players in no doubt what they are up against, he always tells us 'if you play to the best of your ability, you can beat anyone in the country', and that's the attitude we went out with and that's exactly what we proved. Personally,

I was thrilled to come out of the game with a lot of credit and with so many people, Harry included, telling me how well I'd done against one of the best strike forces in the Premiership and, arguably, Europe. I needed that after a period of uncertainty and doubt. But whilst I was pleased that people recognised my performance, it was inevitable that the major talking point afterwards would be the sending off of Arsenal's fiery French midfielder Patrick Vieira for the now infamous spitting incident. It seems as though I got as much credit, more probably, for the way I conducted myself and the restraint I showed than I did for my performance in my first full league game of the season. It was always going to be a hot-blooded affair, London derbies always are, but nobody in their wildest dreams could have imagined how it was all going to kick off with Vieira committing what I described at the time as 'the lowest of the low' dirty tricks you can commit on a football field. He's a hot-headed player, we all know that and we've all seen how he can react on occasions, but it wasn't a deliberate ploy by me or any of the other West Ham lads to wind him up or provoke him as he claimed afterwards.

It was simply a London derby which was played in a passionate, committed manner and Vieira over-stepped the mark in a way that can only be described as disgraceful. We'd had a run-in during the first half when he used a deliberate, professional block to prevent me challenging for a high ball with Tony Adams and I ran into him, knocking him out of the way with a simple body-to-body challenge. It was nothing more, nothing less than that but he started whingeing about an innocent collision, asking me why I had 'attacked' him and there were a few unfriendly words exchanged between us as a result. Both he and Arsene Wenger complained afterwards that I had called him a 'French prat' and whilst I can't remember exactly what I said to him, it was probably something along those lines. But it wasn't a racist comment or anything like that; merely the sort of verbal banter which goes on between players during games in the heat of the moment. I didn't think it was a big deal but if it served to wind him up, and put him off his game then that's his problem. But it didn't turn into a running battle with Vieira, who I happen to rate as a fantastic footballer by the way, and the next contact we had was after he'd been sent off for a second bookable offence and a second foul on Paolo Di Canio. It was suggested that Paolo had dived and Wenger was quoted as saying afterwards that the Italian's behaviour was unacceptable and contributed to Vieira's red card, but that's just sour grapes. It was a crap challenge, and he knows it. Having said that, I would probably have been disappointed if it had been me getting my marching orders for two bookables, but the way games are refereed these days you have to accept that you're treading a fine line with tackles of that nature. I don't like to see players sent off for such things because I believe that it's a man's game and you've got to have physical contact but, by the same token, we know that referees are under pressure to make such decisions and, given today's rules, he probably had to walk.

I could understand Vieira's frustration and disappointment, but what I couldn't understand was his crazed reaction after I'd actually stepped in to try and calm him down and prevent him getting into further trouble. I wasn't too far away when I spotted Vieira, who seemed to have been walking off the pitch calmly, turn round and apparently make a run for the referee. I attempted to block his path but he went berserk and maybe thought I was having a go at him when, in actual fact, I was trying to do him a favour. I've been on the receiving end of a few red cards in my time and know how your temper can get the better of you in those situations and I didn't want him to do something he might regret. Even when he threw an arm out at me I just told him to calm down, to cool it and said words to the effect: 'I'm trying to help you out, you stupid prat.' But he took it the wrong way and was in such a rage by then that, even though Gilles Grimandi was holding him back, Vieira managed to get close enough to me to hit me full in the face with a mouthful of spit. I was stunned for a second and couldn't believe what he'd done. In all my years in football, I've never had anyone spit in my face nor have I seen it happen to anyone else during a game in which I've been playing. It's like an unwritten rule, you just don't do it.

It's the most disgusting and degrading thing a professional footballer can do on the field and I'm amazed how I managed to keep my emotions in check and my temper under control. Immediately after it happened I saw red and wanted to hit him, and a few years ago I would have snapped, taken the player out in no uncertain terms, and no doubt landed myself in hot water as a result. I think most people would have understood it if I had gone for him but incredibly, and despite the fact that in my heart I wanted to punch his lights out, I came to my senses and managed to keep my cool long enough for his teammates to get him out of harm's way … and arm's reach. I did let him have a few choice words as he went off and I gestured towards the dressing room as if to say 'go on, now f*** off' which, under the circumstances, was a fairly meek and mild reaction; certainly by some of my previous standards.

I've been involved in a few scraps and scrapes in my time and done some stupid things which I've regretted almost as soon as I've done them, but I would never, ever stoop so low as to spit in an opponent's face. I would sooner a player kick me, or whack me than resort to something so disgusting, so unnecessary. As I came off the field at the end of the game I made a point of going over to the referee, Mike Reed, to ask him if he'd seen Vieira spit at me and whether he was going to include it in his report. He said he had not seen anything, and neither had the linesman on that side of the field which I find incredible. Everyone inside the ground saw it except two of the three men who were supposed to be running the show. I wasn't trying to make matters worse for Vieira and if he had kicked me off the ball or punched me in the face I wouldn't have gone up to the referee, but this was different. This sort of thing has no place on a football field and, because I was still riled by the whole affair, I wanted the officials to be aware of the fact that a player had committed such a low-life crime.

Bizarrely, when I was interviewed by the BBC straight after the game they didn't even mention the sending off or the spitting incident, preferring to talk about what an exciting game it had been and what an important win it was for West Ham. Typical BBC, I guess. Perhaps they were worried how I might react if they'd asked me a controversial, leading question and the reporter actually asked me after the cameras had stopped rolling if I would have spoken about the spitting incident, and I said I would have done. As I did to the newspaper reporters who were straight on the case, demanding to know what I thought of Mr Vieira once the dust had settled. One paper ran a headline the next day which screamed 'YOU'RE SCUM, VIEIRA' which was not strictly true. What I'd actually said was that it was a 'scum thing' to do, but it came across in a much more aggressive way. I should have known better really.

As far as I was concerned it was all over and I didn't have any bitterness towards the player. I don't think we'll ever be the best of friends and suddenly start 'hanging out' together, but I'm happy to accept that he made a mistake and is genuinely sorry for what he did. I've selected him in my PFA team of the year before and would do so again, purely and simply on his footballing ability which is unquestionable. What happened doesn't change my opinion of him as a player, I still think he's a great footballer, but as a person you have to put a huge question mark over him.

Obviously he was going to get severely punished after that but, as much as I resented him at the time, I would never have suggested that the FA should throw the book at him or anything like that and I was even prepared to accept the apology he put in the papers the next day. That was enough for me. I didn't even want to see him get a lengthy ban because you want players of his calibre out on the field, not sitting in the stands. He still maintained that he was subjected to 'provocation' throughout the game but, as I said before, things like that are part and parcel of football at the highest level and he's got to expect it. I've been provoked in the past but I've never done that. I was amazed to hear on the radio the following day that I was the one to blame because I'd been the 'antagonist' as they called it, but for them to come down on the side of Vieira was almost as outrageous as what he'd done in the first place. I was the victim not the villain, for heaven's sake. He even admitted he was at fault and was prepared to accept his punishment. Worse than any ban from Vieira's point of view, however, is that other players will have seen how he lost the plot and will set out to push him over the edge again in the future. He's got to learn to handle the aggro, handle the pressure; just as I've done – albeit a bit later in my career. I was really pleased with my reaction at the time – amazed, more like – and I think I surprised a few people with the way I conducted myself. Mum and Dad, in particular, couldn't believe the restraint I had displayed. Their little boy has finally grown up. Having said that, I think the main reason I managed to keep my cool was the scoreline at the time. We were 2–0 up and I was in a positive state of mind; I'm sure it would have been a bit different if we had been 2–0 down. I would probably have gone for him under those circumstances, but thankfully I was able to call on my experiences of the past and handle the situation in a mature manner. Even the Arsenal players, especially my old mate Tony Adams who also conducted himself brilliantly throughout, came up to me and said 'well done' for not getting involved and making matters worse. They knew Vieira was in the wrong and what he'd done was unacceptable, as many of them went to great lengths to point out in the players' lounge after we'd hung on for a very satisfying 2–1 win after Davor Suker had pulled a goal back late on. I don't want to name names because I don't want to cause a dressing room rift between Patrick and his team-mates, but they were just as appalled by his actions as I was. It wasn't until then that I realised Vieira had also been involved in an incident in the tunnel as he made his way to the dressing room. I didn't see anything myself but Craig Forrest, our reserve keeper, said that there had been an incident involving Vieira and a police officer although he wasn't sure exactly what went on. To be honest I wasn't interested. I didn't see him after the game and I wish I had; not to take out revenge or anything like that, but just to underline the fact, to his face, that while I might be able to forgive him for what he did in the heat of the moment, I would never forget it.

Once the game had finished and the adrenalin had stopped pumping, however, the result was the only thing which mattered to me. The feeling was absolutely marvellous. We'd beaten a great side, another three Premiership points were in the bag and I'd turned in a solid 90-minute performance. What's more, in a game which was littered with bookings as well as Vieira's sending off, I didn't even get a yellow card from referee Reed who was throwing them around like confetti. I must be going soft in my old age. Seriously, I think the way I handled myself shows how much I've changed, calmed down if you like, in the last few years. It's taken a long while for me to turn the corner but I'm a seasoned professional now and realise it's pointless getting involved and picking up needless bans. Harry Redknapp bought me because he knows I'm a totally committed player, but he also bought me for my experience and I'm no use to him sitting in the stands. I desperately want to repay the faith he showed in me at a time when others were doubting whether I could still hack it at the top level, and I think I've gone some way towards doing that.

I've known Harry for years, always respected him and what he's achieved in the game and it's great to finally be playing for him at what is a magnificent, family club. He's a great coach, a good motivator and a nice man generally, although he's not the 'Happy 'Arry' people might think he is all the time. He loses his rag – as he did when Andy Impey was disgracefully sold to Leicester behind his back last season – like all managers do from time to time; it's the nature of the game, and the nature of a very difficult and pressurised job. But he keeps a happy dressing room and whilst we're allowed to call him 'H' – as opposed to gaffer or boss, as is normally the case – the players have absolute respect for him and we know he's the man in charge; the man pulling the strings. As a manager you have to distance yourself from the players, but he still enjoys a laugh and a joke with the lads and you know full well that his door is always open if you want to go in and discuss any problems with him. If he can help you in any way he will, and that is always nice to know. That's not to say he doesn't lay the law down from time to time, as he did after the Christmas party affair when he was anything but impressed about the adverse publicity we had attracted to his club. But, like most things, he handled that situation well and everything was quickly forgotten about, and it was business as usual.

CHAPTER FOURTEEN

So Near and Yet So Far

Whilst I had always got on well with Harry during the first year or so of my time at Upton Park, things did get a bit heated between us at certain stages of the 1999/2000 season; a frustrating one for me mainly because of injuries. But that's often the nature of a relationship between a fiery manager and a fiery player who both speak their minds. We've got something of a love-hate relationship, me and Harry. It's a bit like a marriage; hot and cold. One minute we hate each other, the next we're the best of friends. He's like that with a few players but you just have to get on with your job. It never bothered me. He would lose his rag with me, I'd lose my rag with him but it was nothing vicious or vindictive and nothing which wasn't forgotten about the next day. Just the sort of thing which goes on at football clubs all the time. It could boil down to something as trivial as me coming in with the hump over something and he could come in with a mood having had a couple of losers at the races the previous day – or Jamie had had a bad game for Liverpool! – and we'd clash. But it was usually forgotten about as quickly as it happened. Our relationship has changed though, mainly because he is one of those managers that when a player is out injured – as I have been quite a lot in the last year – he won't speak to you, but when you're in the team doing well he loves you. When you're doing the business he's the first one to pat you on the back and say 'well done'; if you're injured and no use to him, he'll blank you. Simple as that. Most managers are like that.

I don't think our run-ins had anything to do with the fact that, half way through the season, I was being linked with other clubs here and there. I certainly don't think he'd got the hump with me so bad that he was trying to get rid of me. There were a few inquiries – Nottingham Forest and Charlton were two I heard about – but they were only talking about loan deals until the end of the season and I wasn't interested in that. If I was going to leave West Ham for anyone it would have had to be a decent offer and a permanent deal, but that was never the case. It was a similar situation with Portsmouth just before the transfer deadline. They wanted to take me until the end of the season, but I didn't want to know. I was happy to stay at West Ham, get myself fit and fight for my place in a very competitive squad. There was even talk at one time of my old club Millwall wanting me to go back there and I think a lot of people thought I might take up the option, because that was where I started my career, but again nothing came of it. I said all along that I'd got a year left on my contract at West Ham and was happy to see that out. After that, who knows? To be fair to Harry, he kept me informed of any developments and when clubs made a move for me. He called me in and said that Forest had wanted me on loan and then Portsmouth but there was no pressure on me to go and talk to them and, although I did go home and think about the options, I never fancied a move and he accepted that. He was just doing what all decent managers should do when a club makes an approach; keep the player in the picture and let him know what's going on before someone else does. Often, when a player is looking for a move, the manager doesn't tell him anything – as happened to me earlier in my career at Southampton. But that, as they say, is football.

You're never quite sure what's going on; never quite sure what's around the corner because things can change so quickly in football. I'll always be grateful to Harry for giving me the opportunity to play for a great club like West Ham, in the Premiership, and I was in no hurry to leave. I was still enjoying life at Upton Park, despite the problems and my odd run-in with the manager from time to time.

I think you can put a lot of it down to frustration on both parts. Mine, because of all the injuries and being in and out of the side all season; Harry's, because he had seen our season fall away and his hopes of European football next time fall with it.

Looking back I think that, while the Intertoto Cup campaign – which took place during what would have been a normal pre-season – helped us in the early stages, because the lads were fit and sharp when the league kicked off, it took its toll later on, especially in the last four games when we fell away badly and missed out on a European place. We had been looking at a top six place for much of the season so to blow it at the end – we only picked up one point from our last 12 – was bitterly disappointing. A lot of the players were looking a bit leg weary at the end of it all so, although the decision to go into the Intertoto Cup paid off in the early stages because we got into the UEFA Cup proper, it cost us in the end. And, in hindsight, playing those competitive matches at a time when we'd normally be building up our fitness and playing friendlies probably backfired on me. I'd picked up an injury in the Intertoto, a hamstring initially, and although I came back and played in the UEFA and then had a run in the side, maybe it had a knock-on effect because I was forever picking up niggling injuries after that. A hamstring strain is a funny injury because all week in training you work hard and feel fine but then, when it comes to a match situation, it can go again just like that. Michael Owen had problems with his for a while so if it can affect a kid like him imagine what it's like for an 'old fella' like me. These sort of things can take months to put right, especially when you get the wrong side of 30 and you realise you can't rush back from injuries. You have to be patient, even though that's often been difficult for me in the past. Now, with the benefit of experience, I try not to get too down about these things because you just end up winding yourself up, and everyone around you.

Basically, we were playing competitive football for 10-11 months and because the games were coming up thick and fast there wasn't much chance to rest in between. That sort of schedule is bound to take its toll; it did with me and I know some of the other lads felt the same. That's not to say we shouldn't have gone down that route; it was a case of 'six of one; half a dozen of the other'. That was our only route into Europe and we took it. We eventually lost out to Steaua Bucharest, who were a decent side, so we had a bit of a run and it was all good experience for the younger lads. I was disappointed to have to sit out some of those games and that was the story of my season really. In for a few games, out for a few, on the bench here and there. But, at the end of it all, I still managed over 20 starts in all competitions which wasn't too bad considering all the injuries I'd had and the fact that the team was being chopped and changed around with me, Igor Stimac, Rio and Javier Margas swapping roles from time to time.

It is when the manager has to keep switching the team around that inconsistency starts to creep in and, essentially, that was our main problem last season. We'd string a few decent results together – as we did at the start of the season – and then go on a dodgy run. I can remember reading somewhere, something along the lines of West Ham are back in 'the familiar territory of anything can happen'. I guess the fella who wrote that wasn't far wrong because we were pretty unpredictable at times. Mind you, the fixture list wasn't too kind to us around October – November time and not long after we'd beaten Arsenal (the Vieira incident and all that) we were down to play Liverpool, Leeds and Chelsea in the space of ten days – all away from home! Whoever was responsible for that wants shooting. Liverpool were improving fast, Leeds were top and we all know what Chelsea can be like on their day. So to concede just two goals in those three games wasn't a bad achievement. The fact that we didn't score any and only picked up just one point in the process was another story.

After the goalless draw at Chelsea came another

typically unpredictable result against Sheffield Wednesday; a 4–3 victory at Upton Park against a team that hadn't scored a single goal away from home all season. At least we got a sensible result against Liverpool (1–0) in the next match with Trevor Sinclair getting the winning goal and revenge for the 1–0 defeat we'd suffered at Anfield a few weeks earlier. Christmas and New Year never seems to be a good period for West Ham but, after losing 4–2 at home to Manchester United just before the holiday period, we drew four games on the trot – against Wimbledon, Newcastle, Derby and Aston Villa – which wasn't a bad return by previous standards.

Things were going pretty well in the Worthington Cup too. Although we'd bombed out in the FA Cup – a competition the club hasn't won since 1980, when Trevor Brooking's header sealed our victory – at the Third Round stage to Tranmere, we reached the quarter-finals of the League Cup and were starting to think about a trip to Wembley. But, talk about a spectacular and controversial failure. Even by West Ham standards, the ultimate defeat by Aston Villa was bizarre to say the least.

Having drawn with Villa 2–2 after extra time at Upton Park, we won 5–4 on penalties and were happily celebrating a safe and successful passage into the semi-finals when news broke that we could be forced to replay the tie because we had played an illegible player.

I didn't know anything about it until I heard on the radio that Manny Omoyimni, a young Nigerian lad who'd only made a few first team appearances and who came on for the last seven minutes of the Villa match, had actually played for Gillingham in the same competition whilst on loan earlier in the season. Obviously that made him illegible to play for another club in the League Cup but, while he must have known and remembered he'd played for Gillingham, he wasn't fully aware of the rules of the competition and, therefore, didn't say anything to anyone. The lads, naturally, were upset when it was confirmed that we would have to replay the game but we weren't angry or annoyed with Manny, he's only a kid for heaven's sake, and we certainly didn't blame him or hold him responsible.

If anything, we felt a bit sorry for him, especially when he came into the club a couple of days later and was in tears, poor lad, and apologising to everyone. It was a genuine mistake and the worst you can accuse Manny of was being naïve. Not that the fans were so understanding or forgiving. But the players didn't blame him or hold it against him; it was just an almighty cock-up all round. It was the club who sent him on loan to Gillingham and, presumably, gave him permission to play in the Worthington Cup for them. Therefore, someone, somewhere must have known what the situation was when he returned to the club so you can't just point the finger at Manny. Everyone else concerned should take a share of the blame for that one. Obviously, when we lost the replayed cup tie we were absolutely devastated. We'd already beaten Villa in our view. What difference does seven minutes make? You can imagine then just how Manny felt and I think it was the stick he'd taken in the papers and from the fans that led to the club packing him off on loan to Scunthorpe. Talk about a case of the punishment not fitting the crime. No-one deserves that!

But that was typical of our luck and typical of the way our season was unfolding; folding more like. Had we gone through to the semis we would have met Leicester and, having beaten them home and away last season, we fancied ourselves to beat them over two legs and take our place at Wembley. But it wasn't to be and the subsequent defeat by Tranmere in the Third Round of the FA Cup merely served to rub salt into the wounds, as they say. West Ham's cup curse had struck again.

It was around the time of the first Villa game that I was enjoying my longest run in the team – 11 games in all, including a couple of substitute appearances – and I really started to feel part of things again. But then injury struck again and I was out for three games. Then back for one and out for three. Same old story.

The worst one, a fractured eye socket, ended that run of games. It happened just before half time in the game against Wimbledon on Boxing Day. I banged heads with Carl Leaburn, an accidental aerial clash, and I damaged my eye and he cut the back of his head. I knew there was something wrong at half time because I'd already developed a headache, I was dizzy and felt sick, and the doc recommended that I came off because I was suffering from concussion. I knew it was more than just a bang on the head. But then I remember Harry coming in and saying 'Are you a hard man, or what?'. And that was it, red rag to a bull. That was all I needed to know and I thought 'Right, I'll show you, you b******' and went out for the second half. Not the most sensible thing to do and if Harry had said at the time 'you'd better come off' I would have done, but once he questioned my commitment there was only thing I was going to do. I was still in trouble, my vision was blurred, but I got through the game because I had a point to prove. Yes, I'm a hard man. It wasn't until afterwards when the doc examined me more closely that they realised I had actually fractured my eye socket and they reckon that if I'd taken another blow in the same place I could have lost the sight in that eye. To see what was wrong I had to pinch my nose and blow out of it, as you would on an aeroplane, and my eye socket filled up with air. That's when they knew it was serious and I couldn't open my eye for five days. It could have been a lot worse though.

After recovering from that I picked up an ankle injury, which troubled me for a couple of months and then, to top it all, I damaged the heel on my other leg. It seemed never ending and when you're in and out of the side, as I was, it's difficult to get any consistency in your game and it seemed as though, just as I was getting into my stride, I picked up another knock. I've been out for long spells before with serious injuries and while these problems were not too serious and didn't warrant operations, just treatment and rest, such a catalogue of them hampered me throughout. Not that I moped around feeling sorry for myself; well, not that much anyway. How could I when poor old Stuart Pearce was going through such pain and anguish after breaking his leg for a second time – against Southampton – so soon after he'd come back from the first break against Watford earlier in the season. He was the one people should feel sorry for; not me. But, typical Psycho, he refused to let the latest setback finish him, even at his age (37), and I'm sure he'll be back. He's a great player, great character and a lovely fella to have around the place. And even though he was injured I still used to take the micky out of him on the occasions we saw him while he was recovering. He didn't come in every day, but when he did turn up I used to mock him by saying, 'It must be pay day; Pearcey's in again'. He took it all in good spirit. Having had a few ding-dongs with him over the years as opponents, and not exactly friendly ones either, it was nice to finally be at the same club as him and share a few laughs together. And a few stories. Like the time when I was playing for Southampton (he was at Forest) and we both went into a great 50-50 tackle, which shook the pair of us. It wasn't until he joined West Ham that he admitted he was in a lot of pain, so much so that he was unable to take one of his trademark free-kicks from the edge of the box soon after our almighty challenge. He just walked away. I think he felt a bit better when I confessed that I was hurt too. But both of us were too proud to either show it or admit it at the time. Now, I'd like to think we have a mutual respect for each other.

Going back to last season and, injuries aside, I'm happy that when I did play I did as much as I could do, always gave my all, as ever, and never cheated on anyone. Never have. That's the way I've approached games throughout my career and I'm not going to start changing now. I'll carry on doing that until I hang up the old boots. Hopefully, that won't be for two or three years yet.

I know the fans haven't always been behind me, and I've had some stick from them on occasions, but that's par for the course wherever you play. Supporters are the same all over the country. The relationship between players and fans is like the marriage situation I was talking about earlier; it blows hot and cold. Whenever I mix with supporters after a game or see them away from the ground they have been as good as gold. They might start slagging me off behind my back, but that doesn't bother me. They've never said it to my face, strangely enough. It has never bothered me what people think about me; everyone's entitled to their opinion. I'm too old to start letting things like that worry me.

But, while I only started 12 league games all season (with another few as sub and a handful of appearances in the cups) there were some good moments to look back on. Like beating my old team Liverpool at home and putting one over on my great mate Alan Shearer when we beat Newcastle towards the end of the season. He hates that!

The return against Tottenham, who had beaten us 1–0 on the opening day, represented a good result for us too because we had Steve Lomas sent off early in the game but still came away from White Hart Lane with a goalless draw. That was a good, battling performance by us and showed what we are capable of. The trouble was, we just didn't perform like that often enough and consistency was a problem all season. As we all know, that's the key to success. It's no good turning it on one week and then blowing up the next. You have to be able to string results together and until we can do that on a regular basis we're never going to break into the top six and put ourselves in a position where we can challenge the big boys.

A measure of how far we have to go was blatantly evident late in the season when we went up to Old Trafford to play the champions-elect. United had already beaten us 4–2 at our place so we knew what we were in for. Mind you, we didn't expect what we got – a 7–1 hammering. Unfortunately(!) I wasn't able to play because of the foot injury which had been giving me grief on and off for a while and the defence was severely weakened because we were also without Stimac and Margas. But you still have to give credit to United because they were awesome on the day; well they were after the first twenty-odd minutes, during which time we took the lead and were looking at the best result of our season. What happened after that was simply breathtaking and, as I watched from the stands, I couldn't help but be amazed by the quality of United's play. Even as a West Ham man I had to admire them. What I was witnessing was unbelievable as United came back from a goal behind, found another gear and were unstoppable from then on.

David Beckham, in particular, was brilliant; a joy to watch. Thank God he's English! Shame Ryan Giggs isn't! In fact, all the United players were in a different class and our lads just couldn't live with them after they'd been wounded by our opening goal from Paolo Wanchope who seems to like Old Trafford for some reason. Don't think many of the lads will have the same appreciation of the venue after this. It must be great to play in a team like that. Don't get me wrong, on our day West Ham are capable of approaching something like the sort of slick, clinical football United produced, but the difference is that they do it week in, week out, season after season. That's why they're the best in the country; untouchable right now. And it's hard to see anyone getting near them in the foreseeable future. What makes them such a great team is that, while they have so many fantastic individuals, they all work so hard for each other, as a unit, and are so difficult to play against.

They just have so many outlets when they are going forward; Giggs and Beckham out wide with Keane and Scholes bursting through the middle. And when a move breaks down they are all back, chasing and battling to regain possession. It is the work they put in when they haven't got possession that sets them apart from the rest of the pack. Their work rate, the way they close players down, is incredible. They just don't let the opposition settle and play for a minute. God, don't you hate them!

They do the simple things well and have got the flair players who can turn it on at the drop of a hat. A manager's dream. Everywhere you look there's class: Stam at the back, Keane in midfield, Beckham and Giggs supplying the crosses and Yorke and Cole finishing it off. Perfect.

It must be fantastic for their strikers to have players of that calibre providing the ammunition and it is little wonder Yorke and Cole have scored so many goals between them since they teamed up a couple of seasons ago. You can knock Coley all you like but look at his goals record – for Newcastle and United – and he's up there with the best in the business. It wouldn't surprise me if his goals-per-game ratio was *the* best. They make a terrific partnership and the soul-destroying thing for their opponents is that when they take those two off – as they did against us after the job had been done – they are able to bring on Teddy Sheringham and Ole Gunnar Solskjaer, who scored with his first touch I seem to remember. What can you do? Solskjaer would be in the starting line-up of virtually every other Premiership team yet he's on the bench more often than not for United. When you've got world-class players replacing world-class players you can't go far wrong. They are a credit to themselves and the game and they set the standard the rest have to try and achieve. That's not going to be easy in the short term, not even for the likes of Arsenal, Liverpool and Leeds who are up there in the big bucks league.

It will probably be some time before we're in a position to compete because we simply do not have the financial resources. But what we do have is a whole lot of talent coming through the ranks and the continued progress of young Joe Cole – until his unfortunate leg break – and the emergence of another former youth teamer, Michael Carrick, were some of the plus points from a season which promised so much but, ultimately, delivered so little. Michael, a big midfielder with bags of skill, took little or no time to give an indication of what he is capable of, scoring on his debut in the 5–0 win over Coventry; our biggest win and best performance of the season.

We also managed to secure the signing of Frederic Kanoute who impressed during his loan spell with us and I know Harry was delighted he was eventually able to find the cash to sign the Frenchman on a permanent basis. He looks a class act – a less ungainly version of Paolo Wanchope, if you like. No disrespect to the big fella, who did well to get the boo boys off his back towards the end of the season with a number of goals only he seems capable of scoring. Although we signed Kanoute for around £4.5 million, Harry does not have the luxury of being able to raid the transfer market like that on a regular basis, which is why it is so important we keep producing quality young players and integrate them into the first team, as the manager has done so successfully over the last few years. Frank Lampard and Rio Ferdinand came through the ranks to establish themselves as key members of the first team and now Joe and Michael look set to follow suit. Joey in particular, as I have already said in this book, is a terrific talent who will go on to great things. Having said that, and even if he hadn't sustained such a bad injury when he did, I don't think he was quite ready for England's Euro 2000 squad. Had he been fit, I still believe the tournament would probably have come around a year too soon for him. But, mark my words, he will be knocking on the door of Kevin Keegan's squad by the time the World Cup comes round. I can see him getting a few qualifying games under his belt – a bit like Gazza did before Italia 90 – and then becoming a regular in time for the finals in 2002. I honestly believe he is capable of doing that and then starring on the biggest stage of all.

Yet while I didn't expect Joe to figure at Euro 2000, I was convinced my good pal Trevor Sinclair would be there. I've already spoken of my admiration for Trevor as a player and, after he'd been named in a few England squads in the build up to the Championship, I was convinced he'd be in the final 22; the pre-tournament squad of 28 at least. It was unbelievable that he was left out completely because along with Paolo Di Canio, who Trevor finished runner-up to in the Hammers' Player of the Year award, he has been outstanding for us. He was devastated when he didn't get in the squad and everyone at the club was amazed. Just as we were staggered that Rio was left out of the final 22. Rio's time will come though, whereas Trevor is probably at his peak.

I would have thought he'd be the ideal player to have in your squad for a competition of that nature because he is so versatile. He can play as a wing back on the right or the left; he can play as a more traditional winger on either side; and he can play just behind the front two or even as an outright striker himself. What more do you want in a utility player? How can you leave a player with so many qualities behind? Unless he's upset someone when he's been away with the England squad before – which is unlikely because he's my best mucker at West Ham and would have told me – then I don't know what else he has to do. He asked me towards the end of the season, 'Do you think I'll be in the 28?', and I told him 'Of course you will; you've been different class all season'. And I meant it. I wasn't just buttering him up, I honestly believed he deserved a place in the squad. He certainly had a better season than some of the players Keegan took to the finals. Maybe it's got something to do with the fact that he's not playing for one of the so-called glamour clubs.

If Trevor had been playing for Manchester United, Liverpool or Arsenal then you could have put your house on him going. That's not to say that the likes of Trevor, Rio and Frank can't achieve international recognition as West Ham players, providing the team is doing well. For that to happen, we have to hang on to players of that sort of quality.

Trevor and Rio are great players, we all know that, but if anyone outshone them last season it was Paulo Di Canio. He has been different class and the fans love him. When he's on song, as he was for so much of last season, he gives everyone around him a lift – and a rocket from time to time if they're not pulling their weight – and he has the whole stadium buzzing with excitement and anticipation. He's more than justified Harry's decision – or did some people say it was a gamble? – to sign him and last season he scored one of the greatest goals I have ever seen. The scissor-kick against Wimbledon was absolutely world class. The funny thing is that, all week in the build up to that game, he had been practicing that same volley every day in training and just couldn't get it right. When he wasn't mis-hitting the ball or falling flat on his back, his shots were going over the fence behind the goal, hitting the corner flag, everything but the back of the net. But come the game, the moment when it mattered, he got it spot on. Everything was perfect about it; body shape, angle, balance, power, placement; the lot.

A bit like Trevor not making the England squad, we couldn't believe that Paulo didn't get a mention in last season's PFA Player of the Year awards. He wasn't even in the top six. If there were six better players than him last season then they must have had one hell of a year, that's all I can say. The man was awesome. I think his reputation, and things that have happened to him in the past, went against him. He's a player other players love to hate, and some people have got the impression of him that he's a bit of a whinger, a bit of a diver and a player who can wind opponents up from time to time. As we know from playing against him. But when you work with him week in, week out and get to know the man you can only have respect and admiration for him. Not only is he a great player, he's a great character you cannot help but like. He does some strange things from time to time, and has been known to 'lose it' even in training on occasions, booting balls around in his rage and stomping off the field in a huff, but we love him. When he performs the way he does you are prepared to ignore some of his little idiosyncrasies and tantrums. He's a passionate man, he cares about the game and he wants to be the best. He enjoys the craic and the dressing room banter too, as do all the foreigners – once they settle in, learn the language and understand what the hell we're going on about, that is. Once they've been there a while they start to join in with the fun; in fact Frenchman Marc Keller is probably one of the biggest micky takers in the dressing room. I'll wind him up and he'll do the same to me, normally by saying things like 'Hey Razor, tell your wife to stop phoning me, will you'.

The thing that makes me laugh about the foreign contingent at our club, and it's probably the same at most clubs these days, is that they make out they don't understand something – especially when the manager's having a go – when they actually know more than they are letting on. I remember Harry in training belting out instructions (a rollicking more like) to Javier (Margas) who turned round to the boss and said 'I'm sorry but I don't understand'. At which point Harry shouted out: 'I bet you'd understand if I offered you ten grand a week more'. That sort of thing goes on all the time. The dressing room has been a bit quieter since Wrighty went off on his travels – everyone was gutted when he left, they all loved him – but there's still a good atmosphere around the place, even though we didn't have such a good season. Not that it was a disastrous one.

To finish in the top ten, as the club has done regularly in recent seasons, is no mean achievement. As I keep telling people it wasn't that long ago West Ham were among the favourites to go down and I think the club has made steady progress. Okay, we fell short of our top six finish of the previous season, but there are a lot of clubs of similar stature to West Ham who would settle for finishing in the top half of the table every season without any worries. What's more, the potential is there for the club to go on and build on that. They are building an impressive new stand and, generally, the club is a more attractive one for high-calibre players to join. When you've got people of the quality of Paolo, Rio, Frank and

Trevor around it is understandable for people to want to play for West Ham United. The important thing is that the club keeps hold of players like that to send out the right messages, both to the fans who obviously want some kind of success and players who might consider joining us – if the club can afford them. I'd like to stick around because I've enjoyed my time here and, as long as I'm a West Ham player, I'll give my best and die for the club; just as I've done for all the clubs I've played for.

Apart from the Vieira situation earlier in the season – when I was the innocent party – the campaign was without any real controversies for yours truly; a spot of transfer speculation aside. No sendings off and only four bookings, so nothing untoward there. It was the first time in my whole career that I'd gone through a whole season without getting suspended, so at least I achieved something. But, a year without Razor hitting the headlines for something other than events on the pitch, would be like a British summer without rain. And, sure enough, with the season only just finished I was all over the news pages of the tabloids after a regrettable incident at the Gleneagles hotel in Scotland during what was supposed to be a quiet, golfing break with my pals Alan Shearer and Mike Newell, and their wives. Needless to say, once news broke about a minor altercation in the plush hotel's restaurant one evening, I was made out to be the villain by the press once again. So let me tell you what really happened that night.

We always go to Gleneagles as a group at the end of the season, and this year we were up there in Scotland with comedian Jim Davidson and snooker star Stephen Hendry who have become good friends. As you can imagine it was quite a lively affair and one which, as often happens when mates get together for a few beers, got a little out of hand. Not quite as dramatic as the papers made out but Mike and I did come to blows; very big handbags at ten paces, you could say. It was all over nothing, really. Some food was flicked; a few choice insults traded and then, in the heat of the moment, Mike and I waded in. But it was all over in a flash with everyone saying 'sorry' and hugging each other, full of remorse for what had happened. The sort of thing which often happens to people when they've had a little too much to drink. But because it's Neil Ruddock, in the company of Alan Shearer and friends, then the papers love it. Any opportunity to paint me as the bad guy. It was all blown completely out of proportion and the papers didn't get all their facts right. In fact, it was salsa that was flicked at my wife, not tomato ketchup as reported. Tomato ketchup in the Gleneagles Hotel? Do me a favour! Seriously, if it had been as bad as people were making out then I'm pretty sure that the police would have had something to say about it and we would have been asked to leave what is a fantastic hotel. Neither of which was the case, everything has since been forgotten and we are all still the best of friends. In fact, we have a laugh about it now. As I've said all along, never a dull moment...

Career Statistics

Born:	Wandsworth, South London
Date of Birth:	9 May 1968
Height:	6ft 2in
Weight:	12st 12lb

Joined West Ham United: 30 July 1998, for £100,000

Former Clubs: Liverpool (1993–98, signed for £2.5 million); Tottenham (1992, £750,000); Southampton (1988–92, £250,000); Millwall (1987, £300,000); Tottenham (1986, £50,000); Millwall (1985, from apprentice).

Club Honours: One Coca Cola Cup winners' medal with Liverpool, 1995

International honours: One full England cap v Nigeria, November 1995, four Under-21 caps plus England 'B' and youth honours.

League and Cup Appearance and Goals

Club	Season	League Apps/goals	FA Cup Apps/goals	League Cup Apps/goals	Europe Apps/goals
Millwall	1985–86	0 (0)/0	0 (0)/0	0 (0)/0	0 (0)/0
Spurs	1986–87	7 (2)/0	1 (1)/1	0 (0)/0	0 (0)/0
Millwall	1987–88	0 (2)/1	0 (0)/0	2 (0)/3	0 (0)/0
Southampton	1988–91	100 (7)/9	10 (0)/3	14 (1)/1	0 (0)/0
Spurs	1992–93	38 (0)/3	5 (0)/0	4 (0)/0	0 (0)/0
Liverpool	1993–98	111 (4)/11	11 (0)/0	19 (1)/1	5 (1)/0
QPR	1998–99	7 (0)/0	0 (0)/0	0 (0)/0	0 (0)/0
West Ham	1998–00	39 (3)/2	3 (0)/0	4 (1)/0	*5 (1)/1

Appearances as sub, in brackets.
*Europe – this includes the Intertoto Cup.

Index